From Holocaust Hell to Paradise Village

Dear Bobby,
   We must NEVER FORGET!
      Sand M Schell
Always with love
      Ruth Sax

Try To Remember-
Never Forget

Memoirs of Holocaust Survivor Ruth Goldschmiedova Sax

Sandra Scheller

TRY TO REMEMBER-NEVER FORGET
MEMOIRS OF HOLOCAUST SURVIVOR RUTH GOLDSCHMIEDOVA SAX

Copyright © 2016 Sandra M. Scheller

All rights reserved. No part of this book may be used or reproduced by any means, graphic, electronic, or mechanical, including photocopying, recording, taping or by any information storage retrieval system without the written permission of the author except in the case of brief quotations embodied in critical articles and reviews.

iUniverse books may be ordered through booksellers or by contacting

iUniverse
1663 Liberty Drive
Bloomington, IN 47403
www.iuniverse.com
1-800-Authors (1-800-288-4677)

Because of the dynamic nature of the Internet, any web addresses or links contained in this book may have changed since publication and may no longer be valid. The views expressed in this work are solely those of the author and do not necessarily reflect the views of the publisher, and the publisher hereby disclaims any responsibility for them.

Any people depicted in stock imagery provided by Thinkstock are models, and such images are being used for illustrative purposes only.
Certain stock imagery © Thinkstock.

ISBN: 978-1-5320-0028-7 (sc)
ISBN: 978-1-5320-0029-4 (hc)
ISBN: 978-1-5320-0027-0 (e)

Library of Congress Control Number: 2016911923

Print information available on the last page.

iUniverse rev. date: 12/12/2016

IN MEMORY

To the relatives who lost their lives shot in the street or in the camps needlessly, those who dug their own graves, and those who committed suicide, you will never ever be forgotten. To my grandparents—Siegfried, Sophie, Oskar, and Erna—and to my Dad, thanks for making me.

DEDICATED

To my most-worshipped mother, Ruthie. I have found you to be not just my mom but also my best friend in the universe.

CONTENTS

Foreword ix
Testimony xi
Acknowledgments xiii
Ruth's Words xv
Not So Easy xvii
Trying to Remember xix
September 1939 xxiii

Chapter 1: Born 1
Chapter 2: Invasion 6
Chapter 3: A Crime to Be Jewish 16
Chapter 4: Theresienstadt 18
Chapter 5: Auschwitz 30
Chapter 6: The Artist 36
Chapter 7: Oskar's Tattoo 40
Chapter 8: Gleiwitz 44
Chapter 9: Zamosc Ghetto 48
Chapter 10: Oederan 50
Chapter 11: Reborn 55
Chapter 12: Tribute to Walter Goldschmied 63
Chapter 13: Skeletons in the Closet 65
Chapter 14: Viktor Frankl 66
Chapter 15: Kurt Sax 69
Chapter 16: Not So Nice 75
Chapter 17: The American Dream 76

Chapter 18: Orange Belt Café and Oskar's Market 79
Chapter 19: Living 83
Chapter 20: RIP Kurt 85
Chapter 21: Ruthie's New Life Without Kurt 89
Chapter 22: Reincarnation 92
Chapter 23: Being Honored by So Many 98
Chapter 24: Hail to the Queen 108
Chapter 25: It's Not Your Time 110
Chapter 26: Ruthie's Temple 113
Chapter 27: Who Is Ruthie? 115

Epilogue 119
About the Author 121

FOREWORD

Pepe Romero

When we think about the past, when knights had swords and fought real battles in which many people were killed and injured, the kind of knight I would strive to be is a version of Don Quixote. But instead of a sword, I actually have a guitar, and instead of shooting deadly artillery, I shoot beautiful sounds.

Try to Remember, Never Forget is written like a piece of music, documenting different moments of Ruth's Holocaust experiences so that present and future generations can learn to *never forget*. It passes down the stories of what happened to a happy, beautiful little girl who within one day—March 14, 1939—had everything taken away from her except for a small suitcase. By the time she reached Auschwitz, that suitcase had been taken away too. She faced Dr. Mengele six times and then was transported to a camp where she made bullets and laid electrical cable in the snow. Not knowing she was on the verge of being liberated, she walked through no-man's-land for two weeks. With G-d in her heart and faith in her soul, she did the impossible, reuniting with her father and mother to begin life all over again.

I am very privileged to have been a close friend of Ruth for many years and delight in her inner beauty. Her story offers a powerful message of hope and perseverance in the face of despair, encouraging us to live in peace and harmony with one another and bring joy and love to the world we live in.

Pepe Romero, world-renowned classical and flamenco guitarist

TESTIMONY

Joseph Gonzalez

Try to Remember, Never Forget describes the powerful and intense journey of Ruth Goldschmiedova Sax and her family finding hope and courage to survive in the midst of human cruelty and depravity. Although unsure of what each new day might bring, having been physically robbed of everything, Ruth prayed each night in thanksgiving for the meager blessings she possessed. With her mom by her side—a miracle in itself—she was able to beat the odds, become liberated, and join her father once again.

Sandra's sharing of Ruth's stories is a reminder to an ever-forgetting world that the Holocaust actually happened and that as citizens of the world we must act diligently to assure that this atrocity never happens again. As the composer of *Steal a Pencil for Me*, a compelling film documentary about two people and the power of love to prevail in the midst of the concentration camps, I find it a privilege to personally witness Ruth's journey. Teaching this day and age about the value of each moment and each person, Ruth's story is an incredible inspiration, and she is a role model for our day and age. My family and I join those who will spread the word to *never forget*.

Joseph Gonzalez, composer
Photo by: David Maung

ACKNOWLEDGMENTS

To my sweetest and most wonderful husband, Mark. When you married me, you got a whole bunch of craziness.

To my beloved children, Samuel and Maxwell. You are and always will be the soul of my existence. I hope you have come to realize what an incredible grandmother you have.

To my relatives Karel, Freda, Felix, and Pam Goldschmied (and families), and Vera and David Hartford (and families). We come from the same blood, and I love you with all my heart.

Thank you so much to Daniel Little (our amazing attorney), Ed Callan (my copyright attorney), and his wife, Shirley. David Reicks at Merrill Lynch in San Diego, California, I am so deeply grateful to you. Thank you to the New Life Club of San Diego for your continued gatherings of Holocaust survivors. To Frances Nassau, Max and Rose Schindler, also survivors, this world is a better place because of you, and we stand united to never forget. Zach Hines, Joey Molina, Agustin Castaneda, David Shor, and Steven Spielberg, your support in holocaust awareness is so deeply appreciated. Never stop. Harriet Israel, I could not have found a better person to meet while visiting Theresienstadt.

Thank you, Chaplain Harry Bennett, Minnie Groel, and the wonderful folks at Paradise Village in National City, California. There are not enough words in the universe to describe how great you have been, not just to my mom but also to everyone. Dr. Eric Adler, thank you for keeping my mother alive.

Dana Scott and Patrick Tieng from iUniverse, you have been

my guiding light though this process, holding my hand each step of the way. Thank you so very much.

Thank you, Morgan Lopez, for keeping us safe. Gracias, Luz Medina, José and Sandra Sosa, for listening to me in English and Spanish over and over again.

Vilen Golovko, creator and founder of the Flying Cranes Aerial Trapeze, you have taught me how to fly with broken wings. You are the greatest boss in the world.

Millions of thanks to Jan Craddock and Chris Cutler for editing and keeping me on track. You are angels.

Thank you to my chosen brothers and sisters for your genuine love and support—Pepe, Carissa, Angel, Nefy, Isabella, and Celin Romero; Claudia Tornsaufer; Joseph and Monique Gonzalez; Edward Foster; Robert Shields; Mark Dizik and John Oden; Vira Syvorotkina; Debbie Ray; Johnathan Lee Iverson; Dr. Marina Plon and Isaac Plon; Linda Lassman Lambert; Mingo and Asho; Mark and Nicole Von Gaza Reavis; Jessie Sitar; Lynda Dotson; Gerald Gordon; Steve Goldkranz; Ninel Novikova; Marina Vantskous; Etherial Creator Marcus Platrides; Barbara Sindelir; Ellen Schauer; Heidi Scheller Bender; and Phyllis and Stephen Sax. Thank you to my dearest godchildren Sergey and Oxana Duman, Vika Volchek, Melanie Chy, and Gary Groff. Loving thanks to Ruth's dearest friends Warren Zysk, Glenn Elgin, Nina Welch, Eytan Erez, Jessie Bustamante, Shirley Garske, Morris Lazard, and Abe Motola. Special thanks to Rabbi Scott Melter at Ohr Shalom, San Diego, California, and the wonderful congregation. This world is a much better place because of you. Lastly, I want to thank my ex-boss for showing me what anti-Semitism looks like in our day and age.

RUTH'S WORDS

*G-d created a beautiful world;
only some people make it so miserable ...*

NOT SO EASY

We never talked about the Holocaust when I was a child. For many years, my mother lived with the philosophy that things just fall into place for a reason, and when I was growing up, this was difficult for me to understand. Upon my father's passing, I realized that my mom was more than my mom—she was my best friend. I started to ask her questions, and her answers were so overwhelming that I felt they needed to be shared—if not with the world, then at least with my family and friends.

At times I wanted to give up this book because Ruthie was getting sidetracked. She expected me to know the European cities and the spelling of names that were foreign to me. I found myself having to stop and think about what she said, and then the next morning I would feel lost. Many times she told me that she didn't sleep well because she was up all night thinking about those who'd died for no reason except that they were Jewish.

Listening to her talk about death was the hardest. I have learned that you just do not die of anything except death itself. Many things come close, and what people lived through—emotionally, spiritually, and physically—must have been horrific.

Many of Ruthie's stories can be found on the YouTube channel "Behind Ruth's Eyes." My son Sam Scheller and his friend Scott Diel created these stories.

Ruthie needs to have so many things done for her now. She is in a wheelchair; she needs assistance in personal affairs and medication; and she has her blood checked regularly to maintain proper levels since her pacemaker was put in. But thank G-d she keeps on ticking. Lately I see more of a decline in my mom, and I try to make the most of each second. Dividing my time between writing and Ruthie is tough but very rewarding. Ruthie does not like to get bored. I think she developed this more than ever in Auschwitz where she just stood and waited to be counted.

We take one day at a time and try to focus on one story at a time. The documents were scattered all over the place, and truly it is a full-time job making sure that they are preserved and safe. Ruthie never took the time to organize the photos and the documents. She was quite amazed at what was found, sometimes staring at a photo for hours on end and saying nothing. I believe she was trying to breathe life into each photo of the relatives who have passed on, mostly her parents.

As I look at other families and situations, I don't think I could have picked a more wonderful mother.

TRYING TO REMEMBER

Great-Grandmother
Klara Goldschmied:
died in Auschwitz,
May 18, 1944

Great-Grandfather
Josef Goldschmied:
died in Auschwitz,
May 18, 1944

Children:

- Oskar, born November 5, 1898; died in San Diego August 10, 1988; one child, **Ruth Goldschmiedova Sax,** born July 6, 1928
- Vilem, born June 10, 1897; died in Zamosc, a small village in Poland, April 28, 1942, with wife Kamila and children Gideon and Nehemias[1]
- Walter, born July 5, 1907 (wife Hildaguarde); died in 1946 one month after a car accident that left his back broken; two children, Karel and Felix
- Zikmund, born June 19, 1903; died in Zamosc April 27, 1942[1]

---

[1] Vilem, his brother Zikmund, and his wife and children were all forced to dig their own graves before they were killed.

Great-Grandmother
Netty Kohn:
born February 7, 1878;

died in Terezin,
April 2, 1943

Great-Grandfather
Frantz Kohn:
born in Nikolov,
Czechoslovakia,
date unknown;
died in WWI in Italy

Children:

- Erna, born March 14, 1906, died in San Diego February 27, 1982; one child, **Ruth Goldschmiedova Sax,** born July 6, 1928
- Manfred Kohn; two children, Vera and Franta
- Elfie Pfefer; one child, Dita

My mother's notes

```
JOSEF GOLDSCHMIED      CZECHOSLOVAKIA   AUSCHWITZ
                       1-29-1870 - DIED 5-18 1944    TEREZIN - AUSCHWITZ FAMILY LAGER
KLARA GOLDSCHMIED      7-26-1868   "    "   "AUSCHWID.    "        "    "     "
VILÉM GOLDSCHMIED      6-10-1897 A 4-28-1942 ZAMOŠČ   TEREZIN, ZAMOŠČ
                                     DIED POLAND
KAMILA GOLDSCHMIED              4-24-1942 DIED ZAMOŠČ   TEREZIN ZAMOŠČ
NEHEMIAS GOLDSCHMIED   2-7-1928 - DIED 4-28-1942 ZAMOŠČ  TEREZIN, ZAMOŠČ
GIDEON GOLDSCHMIED     2-19-1924 - DIED 4-28-1942 ZAMOŠČ  TEREZIN - ZAMOŠČ
ZIKMUND GOLDSCHMIED    6-19-1903 DIED 4-27-1942 ZAMOŠČ  TEREZIN - ZAMOŠČ
VITEZSLAV PFEFFER      9-21-1888 - DIED 7-22-1942 TEREZIN   TEREZIN
NETTY KOHN             2-7-1878  DIED 4-2-1943 TEREZIN  TEREZIN

ALSO FAMILY MEMBERS, LILLY SUCHACITA, ERNST SAX HERTA DIED TYPHOID IN TEREZIN
FRITZ KRAKAUER, SAM KRAKAUER, OLGA KOHN, AND MANY OTHERS, PAULY ADLER

                                                      1941    1944   1944-45    1945
RUTH SAX/GOLDSCHMIED LIVING   07-06-1928 CZECHOSLOVAKIA  TEREZIN, AUSCHWITZ-OEDERAN TEREZIN
KURT SAX         LIVING  08-24-1922 AUSTRIA  LEFT 1939 TO ITALY AND THEN U.S.A.
                                                                                    OEDERAN
ERNA GOLDSCHMIED     03-14-1906 CZECHOSLOVAKIA. DIED IN SAN DIEGO CA. TEREZIN AUSCHWITZ TEREZIN
                                                              8-10-1985
OSKAR GOLDSCHMIED    11-05-1898 CZECHOSLOVAKIA DIED IN SAN DIEGO TEREZIN AUSCHWITZ BLECKHAMER
```

Oskar's notes

2. Dec. 1941 interniert werden
5 Dec 1941 Ghetto Terezin
23 Okt 1944 Transport Auschwitz
27 Okt 1944 to Oederan - Germany
11 April 1945 Todesmarsch mit Train
              to Terezin
21. April   Ankunft in Terezin
20 Juni   Aufenfl in Jena

Was in e typhoid quarantine

─────────────────────────────

VERLASSEN
LEFT   Č.S.R, 16 AUGUST 1949
ANKUNFT IN NEW YORK. U.SA OCTOBER 4,1949

─────────────────────────────

Landesversicherungsanstalt # 5422

1945. My grandfather, Oskar, visits the graves of his grandparents born in the early 1800s in Pohořelice, Czechoslovakia.

SEPTEMBER 1939

September 1
Germany invades Poland, initiating World War II in Europe.

September 3
Honoring their guarantee of Poland's borders, Great Britain and France declare war on Germany.

September 17
The Soviet Union invades Poland from the east.

September 27
Warsaw surrenders. In the days that follow, the Polish government flees into exile via Romania, and Germany and the Soviet Union divide Poland between them.

TRY TO REMEMBER

Written by Tom Jones for the musical *The Fantastiks*

The kind of September
When life was slow and oh so mellow.
Try to remember the kind of September
When grass was green and grain was yellow.
Try to remember the kind of September
When you were a tender and callow fellow.
Try to remember and if you remember
then follow ... follow ...

CHAPTER 1

Born

Ruth Goldschmiedova was born in Moravsky Šumperk Moravia, the central region of Czechoslovakia, on July 6, 1928. In our numerous interviews, I asked her what life was like before she heard the name *Hitler*. She replied, "Life really was beautiful growing up as an only child, and I was very spoiled." Ruthie remembers back to when she was three years old and a dog bit her. As a result, even as a young adult, she was afraid of dogs. As of this date, she has learned to love my dogs as they love her.

She told me something that had me in stitches. As a child, she saw the very religious Jews wearing black when going to temple, and so she figured all black dogs were Jewish.

My mom at about five years old with Elsa, the nanny

My grandparents lived in a comfortable loft apartment behind their shop. As a young child, Ruth had a nanny named Elsa and numerous friends, both Jewish and non-Jewish. There were times when she wished she had a brother or sister, but as she explained, she enjoyed being spoiled by numerous family members.

Chances are that if she'd had brothers or sisters, they would not have survived the camps. To have a family unit survive as my mom and grandparents did is unbelievable. They did the impossible.

I asked my mom when she first heard the name *Hitler*. She replied that when she was ten years old, things began to change. The non-Jewish neighbor children were afraid to play with her, and her parents told her that if she loved her friends she would let them go because bad things could happen to them. As my mom tells me these stories, she shows very little emotion. It's all very factual.

Oskar and my mom. These photos were taken before the Holocaust and saved by my mother's aunt Gartie, who was married to my grandfather's brother, Walter. Walter survived the Holocaust but unfortunately died months later in an accident on a bridge that collapsed. He broke his neck.

Try To Remember-Never Forget

One thing about my mom is that she has such an appreciation for life even to this day. Ruthie is in a wheelchair because of her numerous back surgeries and fusions. She has almost died five times in eight years, and yet she beats the odds. She has an incredibly sharp mind, and I can only imagine the strength she had as a young child and what she had to do to survive this horrific ordeal.

Who would have thought that Ruthie would survive concentration camps, six confrontations with Dr. Josef Mengele, a death march, a typhus quarantine, and then beginning life at the age of seventeen without a dime. I never knew the details when I was growing up because it was something we just did not talk about. Maybe she thought that, as children, we were not interested or that the ordeal was too painful to share with us.

As I talk with my mom, I am shocked and amazed at the things she tells me with a smile on her face. Not once has she broken down telling me stories—but then, I see that she has her children to live for. I do remember when I was about ten years old, hearing my mom scream early one morning. I ran into her room, and my dad was comforting her. He told me my mom had a nightmare, and I should just to go back to sleep. My dad, Kurt, loved my mom dearly, but many times he treated her like a child. He made the decisions in the family, and he kept her very protected to make sure she would not feel any pain.

Ruthie was both physically and emotionally damaged, yet she made it her mission to never let on. She had hope, and as long as there was hope, there was tomorrow. Tomorrow would be a new day. Her tomorrows turned into years, but still she had hope, and this was her strength.

In the camps, as long as my mom was working, she got eight hundred calories a day. If she didn't work, it was three hundred. I'll mention now that my mom was not tattooed or raped, but she was shaved everywhere. Tattoos were given to those in Auschwitz, but she and my grandmother were not there long enough to receive one. Oskar did, as I will describe later in the book.

Back to Ruthie's childhood. The family moved to Brno when Ruth was six years old, but Elsa stayed behind. She helped her dad on the family fox farm and continued her studies. She did visit my mom before the invasion, but after the camps, Elsa was never seen again. As I am sitting with Ruthie now, she is bowing her head in the hope that she will still see Elsa one day.

This is in Pohorealiza, Czechoslovakia, not far from Brno. Over to the right, you will see Hotel Adler. From the hotel all the way back belonged to my grandfather's family. This is where Ruthie spend her summers.

The shops are on the bottom, and the living was on the second floor.

Ruth at about five years old in the family garden

Around the time my mom was eight years old, she took violin lessons from a very strict violin master. Her father played violin, his father played violin, and her mother played piano. Little Ruthie was very upset with her teacher because every time she played a wrong note, he would hit her with his bow on her little delicate hands.

One day she got very ill with scarlet fever, and the choices were to go to the hospital or hire a private nurse. The family hired a private nurse. As Ruthie got better, she became very jaundiced and yellow. Her mom surprised her by taking her to a toy store. There her mom said that she could have anything she wanted—just name it. Little Ruthie said that she never wanted to take another lesson again, ever. This wish came true.

After the war, she noticed that her aunt had saved her violin. As we talked, we realized that had the invasion been sooner or had she got sick in the camp, she would have been killed.

My mom harmonized with those using the toilet.

CHAPTER 2

Invasion

1938 Praga Piccolo

On March 14, 1939, the family celebrated my grandmother's birthday with a beautiful cake. While they fiddled with the radio trying to find nice music, an announcement came on that Hitler was going to occupy Czechoslovakia. Knowing that he was out to get every Jew, the family ran downstairs, called a cab, and went to the factory where Oskar worked because there was nowhere else to go, and Oskar was most concerned about his job. The owner of the factory was Jewish.

When the family showed up, the director of the factory greeted them, and Oskar noticed that the man now had a swastika on his lapel. Oskar was in complete shock to see that his supervisor was a Jew hater. My grandfather was told to "*Go home!*" The years of friendship and friendliness had turned into a fireball of hatred just like that.

They tried to take another cab home, but the driver drove them to the train station because he was afraid to have Jews in his cab. The trains still allowed Jews to travel, so they returned home that way.

When they finally reached their front door, two German SS officers with revolvers greeted the family and demanded to enter their home. Ruthie remembers that the family was escorted outside the door, and the Germans began to help themselves to whatever they wanted. She was too young to remember what was taken. The crystal in the cabinet was still intact, but she remembers Oskar handing over the keys to his brand-new car. She reminds me that it is hard to remember the details. Maybe at this stage in her life, it is for the best.

She does remember that her parents were very nervous. My grandfather was most upset because he needed a car to continue to work, and he didn't know what he would do. The future was their biggest concern. Later on, of course, there was no need for a car because they had been placed in the camps.

My grandfather told one of his customers, who was not Jewish, that the Germans had taken his car. The customer went to the Germans and was able to get the car—not for Oskar, but for himself. He told the Germans that Oskar had sold the car to him. My grandparents were determined to give as little as possible to the Germans, so they gave everything away to people they knew. This was day one of the invasion, so the Nazis had a lot to learn about keeping a good *Jude* down.

Ruthie was robbed of her friends, and being labeled as a *Jude*, she was about to face six years of Nazi hell. She wondered how all these people suddenly had German flags and swastikas. This happened all in one day, and swastikas were everywhere. She even remembers seeing them on the houses of Jews. She never knew so many swastikas existed; she could not believe they were everywhere and had been put up so fast.

The family had a non-Jewish cook named Maña. Mom said that she was an amazing cook. Maña was forced to leave the family because she was not Jewish, and she worked for Germans. My mom was unhappy about losing Maña because she had been part of the family for so many years.

After the war, Mom ran into Maña, and although she was happy to see her old cook, she had a huge issue with trusting anyone non-Jewish. Maña invited my mom to visit, but her emotional wounds still needed healing, and she had to learn to communicate with people again without being afraid or asking for permission. To this day, I see that when Ruth meets people, she looks at them for quite some time before saying anything. Maybe it's a good thing.

My mom had a gold necklace that meant so much to her; her grandmother Klara had given it to her when Ruthie was only a year old. There was no way that she was going to give this to a Nazi, so she gave it to her dear friend Jirina with no expectation of having it returned. Jirina and my mom walked to school together and marked every celebration together. When Ruthie came back from the camps, she saw her friend, and the first thing Jirina did was give the necklace back. They continued their friendship as though nothing had happened.

As they got older, Jirina continued her education while Ruthie was on her way to get married and come to America. They did continue to write letters but eventually lost contact. To this day, I see that my mom misses her friend dearly.

Ruthie had to get used to many changes quickly. Stores could sell to Jewish people only between three and five o'clock in the afternoon. Jews were given a Star of David with the word *Jude*. They were each given two of them. The stars were to be pinned on every day, and if you traveled without your star, you took the risk of getting injured or killed. Each week, additional rules were put in place for Jews. One week, it was no movies; another, no theaters. Cigarettes and groceries were rationed. Jews could ride on the back of the trolley only. They lost their jobs or had their businesses taken over. Jews were banned from public schools and universities, and eventually the Germans shut down everything for Jews.

The Sudetenland, the "twenty-five-mile bread crust" as my mom describes it, was now occupied by Hitler, and Jews were forced into ghettos. My relatives were forced out of their homes, but luckily my mom and grandparents were able to stay in their place because it was paid for by the factory that my grandfather was associated with—although later on, they were forced to register and then were placed in the camps.

It is difficult as I watch my mom look through photos and documents that have been put in boxes and locked up for at least fifty years. Ruth has such a great memory, and as she stares at these pictures for hours, I see youth lost. The remarkable thing is that she still has hope of finding everything and everyone in her life. I truly believe that when she passes, her parents, her husband, and Elsa will greet her. It is an eventuality I do not want to think about, but I have to be realistic. This makes me want to do anything and everything for her while she is in her paradise on earth.

As a child, my mom loved ice cream. In the same building as her apartment was an ice cream shop called Olivete's. She remembers back to when she was seven years old and her cousin (and later on her husband), Kurt, was visiting the family for the first time. He was studying for his bar mitzvah. If Kurt didn't like what my grandmother told him to do, he would disappear, and he could always be found in the ice cream shop downstairs.

Now, don't think that my mom was a completely well-behaved child. I remember her telling me about one incident involving an outing planned by her grandfather Joseph, who was so proud to be with all the grandkids. He wanted to show off by having an outing with all the grandchildren and take them to the museum. Mom had been to this museum so many times and just didn't want to go again, so off she strolled without telling anyone. Her grandfather was distraught and very upset to have lost her only to find that Ruthie had run home and was with her mom. Ruthie was now forced to stand in the corner. One thing about my grandmother, she never ever laid a hand on my mom, although my grandfather did show his knuckles now and then.

Down the street from Olivete's was a gourmet ice cream shop called Sedlachek. Every day they had an ice cream flavor called "the Secret," and it changed daily. The idea was to go in, get a sample, and then figure out what the ice cream was. The ice cream also came with beautiful edible decorations. It is funny watching Ruth lick her lips now as she describes this dessert eatery.

It was no big deal to walk down the street and visit this "house of sweetness," but one day when my mom was ten years old, she went to this shop only to find a sign saying "Jews Forbidden." There was no way that Ruthie would go into this shop for fear of getting hurt or killed.

After the war, she was able to enter the shop again, but she explained that it was just never the same. Everything was on ration; there were no decorations, the portions were smaller, and something was just missing.

No, Ruthie, it will never be the same for lots of things. But one thing's for sure—she has coffee ice cream almost every day at Paradise Village, where she lives.

Cousin Viktor Fuchs, 1939

My grandfather Oskar had a cousin, Viktor. Every Saturday, they would get together and drink coffee at a local coffee shop. My mom remembers the day that Viktor was walking down the street, minding his own business, and a German walked up to him and yelled, "You dirty Jew!"

Viktor reacted by spitting on this German. The German took out his revolver and shot Viktor dead. That was the first shooting in the city. It happened in front of the building where he lived. My mom lived across the street.

Viktor was a salesman, and his wife was an opera singer. She was sent to Terezin and sang there. The day after the liberation in Bergen Belsen, she died. She was very skinny and exhausted, and she just didn't make it.

I asked Mom how she learned about what had happened to Viktor. "Family members saw it and ran to the house to tell us," she said. "And he was such a nice man."

My family was about to be labeled. Each member of the family was given two stars. There was no Velcro back then, so trying to figure out how these would attach was a problem. The solution was to sew the stars to her favorite jacket and a coat. Ruthie never left home without wearing one or the other.

To this day, we have the stars safe in a box so that Ruthie can share her experiences and let people touch, feel, and yes, even smell them.

The Goldschmieds wore this star on their clothing. You could not travel without it, and if you did, you could be beaten or even killed. Little Ruthie was about ten or eleven years old, and the family went to a Jewish Community Center in Brno. In the past, my mom remembered going to this building, playing with her friends, and learning Hebrew. There was even an orphanage in the back of the building.

Mr. Polaroid

Okresní politická správa v u Šumperku.
Politische Bezirksverwaltung in Mähr. Schönberg.

Číslo: *7860/?*
Zahl: *1927*

List živnostenský.
Gewerbeschein.

Podle § 13. živnostenského řádu potvrzuje se tímto, že:
Es wird hiermit gemäß § 13 der Gewerbeordnung bestätigt, daß:

majitel živnosti: *Goldschmied Viktor*
Gewerbeinhaber:

rok narození: *1798*
Geburtsjahr:

bydliště: *v Šumperku,* *Třída...*
Wohnort: Mähr. Schönberg,

řádně ohlásil samostatné provozování živnosti;
seinen eigenberechtigten Betrieb des Gewerbes:

Pekařství krátkým a běžným zbožím dle § 1b63 živn. řádu
Bäckerei mit Kurz- und Galanteriewaren gemäß § 1b63 der Gew. Ordg.

stanoviště živnosti: *v Šumperku,* *Třída...*
Standort des Gewerbes: Mähr. Schönberg, *Marktplatz čís. 1*
ordnungsmäßig angemeldet hat.

Tato odpověď byla v seznamu svobodných — řemeslných živností
Diese Anmeldung wurde in dem bei der oben bezeichneten Behörde geführten
vedeném u svrchu zmíněného úřadu ve svazku *I* oddělení *aa*
Register über freie— handwerksmäßige Gewerbe im Bande Abteilung
pod běžným číslem *953* zanesena.
unter der fortlaufenden Zahl eingetragen.

v Šumperku, dne 22. VI. 1927 192
Mähr. Schönberg, am

Rada politické správy:
Der Rat der polit. Verwaltung:

Try To Remember-Never Forget

Harry Mahler was the man who employed my grandfather in Brno. Here is the employment document detailing his title. My grandfather represented stockings that had elastic around the leg. Just think, you didn't need garters anymore! My mother talked so highly of this man, and my grandfather had such respect for him.

Mr. Mahler had a hobby—photography. Every year he went to the conventions in the USA to learn and show his work in photography. As Mr. Mahler continued his inventions, he developed the film used in Polaroid cameras. Mr. Mahler wanted to move to the United States. I'm sure he was quite aware that being Jewish and living in Brno/Prague was going to be difficult if not death for him.

He met some folks who bought his patent for this film for the sum of $20,000. At the time, this was quite a bit of money. Mr. Mahler needed a good attorney. I have researched on the Internet trying to find more information about Mr. Harry Mahler. I can't find any, although I would never doubt my mom. Welcome to America, Mr. Mahler.

Years later, my grandfather needed proof of his employment. As we were going through the documents, my mom was laughing with joy as she remembered this delightful man who did so much for the family. This gentleman was so official about everything. All of the letters had neat stamps on them, and every "T" was crossed and every "I" dotted.

It has been a blessing to come upon these documents and be able to take the time with Ruth and see her reaction. Believe it or not, there are documents that she had no idea what they were. We have tried to find out what they are and with some luck have been able to get the gist of what they mean. One thing is for sure—the documents make it clear that my grandparents were incredible workers and they should be employed.

CHAPTER 3

A Crime to Be Jewish

Sigmund Freud

Albert Einstein

Some of the greatest artists, doctors, scientists, university professors, and educators were Jewish. Hitler was willing to stop the world from learning because of those who were Jewish. He rose to power in 1933, and his dislike for Jews was immediately apparent. He ordered Germans to investigate every Jew possible using school records, synagogue records, taxes, and mostly the list of Jewish Community Centers. There were many mandatory registrations, but I believe my mom was just too young to know about them.

Ruthie loved school and her Jewish social outings with her friends, but eventually education was no longer an option for her as her Jewish school had been converted into a Jewish registration center. Jewish students were thrown out of universities so that Hitler could tell students what he wanted, what his plans were, and what to build. Ruthie also explained that neighbors ratted to authorities about Jews living in the neighborhood. Even in the schools, Jewish children were placed in front of the classroom and forced to stand as things that were said to make them different from the non-Jewish students were pointed out. Nothing was done about non-Jewish children belittling and bullying the Jewish children, but then, Jewish children were soon no longer accepted at all from elementary to university levels of education.

Max Planck, a German physicist, asked Hitler to let Jewish scientists keep their jobs. Hitler replied, "If the dismissal of Jewish scientists means the annihilation of contemporary German science, then we shall do without science for a few years."

To this day, I find that I am in absolute amazement at what Hitler did and how he got away with so much. Sometimes I have dreams that I could get a sneak peek into what life was like as a Nazi and how they were so royally treated. I wonder if we can ever recover the damage even in our lifetime from what Hitler did. Today I am the lucky one because I am holding my mom, talking to her, and knowing that she did beat the odds. I am loved, and so is she.

CHAPTER 4

Theresienstadt

Visiting Theresienstadt in 2009

December 2, 1941, began with the Goldschmied family getting their notice that, as Jews, they needed to register at the local school. Everyone was given a number. The notice explained that they were to collect their essential items in no more than two suitcases each and have them at the ready. They could not have more than forty kilos in each suitcase. Ruthie packed her undies, bras, stockings, and even sardines.

When they returned home, their landlady, who had turned

Nazi, harassed them. Every day, she made it a point to ask, "Are you out yet?"

As my mom told this story to me, I could see that she still was not convinced at that time that there truly were evil people in the world. After all, she was only thirteen. She was cute as a bug, came from hardworking parents, was spoiled rotten (as she told me), and was seeing things change in front of her daily.

Three days later, on the night of December 5, 1941, two Germans in their twenties or thirties escorted the family onto a transport wagon. They had their packed bags and also wore three coats, three outfits, three sets of undergarments—anything they could get on their body. The transport was K, and they were numbers 3, 4, and 5. They kept their clothes on, slept on the floor, and were given soup, coffee, and bread. They had been told they would be given a cup, but they had to bring their own utensils.

When the transport stopped, they had to walk about two miles to a train station. They carried their suitcases, and as they arrived, they were greeted by transport trains with open roofs that had probably been previously used to carry animals. The train ride took about a day. The transport was long and crowded with many stops.

Finally, the train stopped in Theresienstadt. Ruthie knew nothing about this place. She was not separated from her parents, but anything valuable was taken away immediately and thrown into barrels and piles on the ground. There were barrels for wedding rings, eyeglasses, and shoes. Gold teeth were pulled out as well. As people passed away, even they were placed neatly in rows, but eventually as the grounds filled with people, they were cremated.

I asked my mom, "What happened if someone needed their glasses?" She told me that chances were, if they could not see without them, they were no good for working, and people were killed for this very reason.

Now the greatest treasure my mom had was taken from her— her dad. There were five barracks in Theresienstadt. Oskar lived in Sudeten Kaserne, while Ruthie and Erna went into the Dresdner

Kaserne. This would be home to the Goldschmied women for three-and-a-half years. There were bedbugs in every room. Ruthie hated these bedbugs. She wondered why they put Czech soldiers into the building after the war.

Of all the camps, this was probably the friendliest, if you could even use that word. Being separated from Oskar was the worst because she loved her dad—and yes, her mom equally. The love between Oskar, Erna, and my mom was infectious. My mom called my grandparents every day to say good morning and good night. I believe they prayed together over the phone.

The town of Terezin was originally built in 1780 by Emperor Joseph II of Austria and named after his mother, Empress Maria Theresa. Terezin consisted of the Big Fortress and the Small Fortress.

The Nazis designed Theresienstadt so they could fool the Red Cross into believing that this was a camp of culture instead of the horrific torture ghetto it later became famous as. Overcrowding, disease, and lack of food were serious concerns. But in many ways, life and death within Theresienstadt became focused on the frequent transports to Auschwitz.

The Nazis had sent approximately 1,300 Jewish men on two transports to Theresienstadt on November 24 and December 4, 1941. These workers made up the *Aufbaukommando* (construction detail), later known in the camp as AK1 and AK2. They were sent to transform the garrison town into a camp for Jews. The largest and most serious problem these work groups faced was changing a town that in 1940 held approximately seven thousand residents into a concentration camp that needed to hold about thirty-five thousand -to sixty-thousand people. At one time, there had to be room for seventy-five thousand, and people were doubling up in beds.

Jews established a *Judenrat* (Jewish Council). Besides the lack of housing, bathrooms were scarce, water was severely limited and contaminated, and the town lacked sufficient electricity. To solve these problems, to enact German orders, and to coordinate the day-to-day affairs of the ghetto, the Nazis appointed Jakob Edelstein as the *Judenälteste* (Elder of the Jews). My grandmother knew him well. We found out later on that he died in Auschwitz on June 20, 1944.

As the Jewish work groups transformed Theresienstadt, the existing population looked on. Though a few residents attempted to give the Jews assistance in small ways, the mere presence of Czech citizens in the town increased the restrictions on Jews' mobility. There would soon come a day when the Theresienstadt residents would be evacuated and the Jews would be isolated and completely dependent on the Germans.

Ruthie, at age thirteen, was forced to grow up very fast. The Germans only kept you alive if you were between the ages of eighteen and thirty-eight. They did not tolerate the weak. They wanted strong working people with professions. So Ruthie lied about her age. How many thirteen-years-olds can hold a job, let alone look like they are eighteen or older? Ruthie did it. I asked her if she stuffed her chest or wore makeup. She laughed because every time the Nazis wanted you to work in a field or wanted anything, you were naked, so stuffing a chest just didn't work. I remember my mom telling me that when she did not feel well, her mother hit her cheeks to give her that rosy glow.

Early one morning, Germans came into the barracks and told everyone to get up and go to the field at the edge of the camp. My mother realized that all the Jews who were in the field were just standing. They just stood there for hours, all day, standing and standing. She didn't have a clue what was going on. During this time, a priest walked by and noticed that the Jews just standing there was out of the ordinary.

Rumor has it that he mentioned at his church what he had seen earlier that afternoon. Toward the beginning of the evening, the Germans allowed the Jews to return to the barracks. Rumors got to my mom that a German officer had been killed, and in retaliation, they were going to wipe out the Jews in Terezin. My mom believes that this priest saved the lives of so many Jews.

Further research reveals that Reinhard Heydrich, one of the

main architects of the Holocaust under Hitler, was killed in Prague on May 27, 1942, by a British-trained team of Czech and Slovak soldiers who had been sent by the Czechoslovak government-in-exile to kill him. He died from his injuries a week later.

Intelligence falsely linked the assassins to the villages of Lidice and Lezáky. Lidice was razed to the ground; all men and boys over the age of sixteen were shot, and all but a handful of women and children were deported and killed in Nazi concentration camps. Many historians regard Heydrich as the darkest figure within the Nazi elite. Adolf Hitler described him as "the man with the iron heart." Rumor has it that he had Jewish ancestry in him and was bullied because of this and his high-pitched voice. At this point, I will mention that Hitler had Jewish ancestry as well.

If you were a German and got pregnant, this was a big deal and a good thing because to donate a child to Hitler was a gift to the Nazi cause. A uniform meant a lot to the Germans. Between the flags and the uniforms, Nazis just could not be decorated enough. The more stripes they had, the more Jews they killed.

My mom remembers two Jewish women who got pregnant in Terezin. As people got together, they made it a point to watch out for one another, but there were no condoms or such to assist with what little fun they found. The women were transferred to Auschwitz, but they did not show. They continued to Oederan, where they worked in the ammunition factory.

A supervisor who oversaw the women's work noticed that they were pregnant. They were supposedly shipped off to work at a much easier camp. But after the war, only one lady survived, and she was without her child. My mom bumped into her on the street, and she explained to my mom that once she delivered her child, the child was taken away and placed in another camp. This dear woman never saw her child again.

I asked Ruthie about her fears, and naturally, she had many. But she felt encouraged when she ran into her dear friend Fredy Hirsch, a physical fitness guru back in Brno. He was in the transport before Ruthie's and advised Erna to volunteer to peel potatoes. He explained that there would always be food because you could eat the peels on the job. The peels would be used for soup. *Everything* was soup. It was either a powder mixed with water or potatoes from the garden that my mom worked in.

Erna worked her way up to supervisor. I asked if Erna had special privileges for getting more food, but apparently she felt guilty if she took more than her share. My grandmother traded pieces of food for more coal, which kept the kettles alive. After she closed down the kitchen for the evening, my mother and grandmother—along with Mom's aunt Elfie and cousin Dita—bathed in the potato water.

This is the children's garden where Ruthie worked.

My mom worked in the children's garden growing vegetables for the Germans. G-d forbid my mother took anything; even a carrot could have been the end of her life. My mom explained that she was under house arrest for a week and could not work because she got caught shaking an apple tree. She told me that in the summertime, she would remove her shoes so she could feel the water on her feet, and in the wintertime she wrapped them in a piece of wrapping paper that she found.

My grandmother was notorious for saving wrappers that she peeled off cans. She would wet the wrappers and smear the red dye on my mom's face to make Ruthie look older, or to make someone who was ill look healthy.

My mother was one of the lucky ones because throughout her concentration camp years, she was able to remain with her mother, although her father was taken away from Theresienstadt and transferred to Auschwitz.

With so much work for my mom and her mother, there was no time to think about her life, Brno, family, etc. Erna's mother had cancer, and she was buried in Terezin. Word got to my mother that the non-Jews who lived in Terezin traded their homes for the beautiful homes that were owned by the Jews in Brno and Prague. My mom said that she heard many of these non-Jews did return to Terezin later for the tourist opportunity.

Many years ago, my husband and I had the opportunity to visit Terezin. Between the tears and the prayers, we were most appreciative of the way the camp had been preserved. It was most eerie to see the toilets, the crematorium, and the beds—even the graves of my great-grandparents. Without anyone looking, I reached down and picked up dirt and placed it in my pocket. My plans are that when my mom passes, she will have soil that covered her grandmother.

In Terezin, my mom wore her own clothes, but it was the same thing day in and day out. She was given coupons and every year was able to pick up a piece of clothing that was left behind by someone who had passed.

My cousins Felix and Karel Goldschmied came to visit me, and they said that when they were young, in the middle of the night they would go with their mom to the edge of Terezin and slip suitcases to someone. Karel, maybe four years old at the time, and Felix, maybe seven, remembered being watch guards for their mom. They avoided the camps because their mom hid them, and my mom explained that Gardie had papers saying she was not Jewish.

Mom said that once a year they were allowed to receive a package, and Aunt Gardie always sent something which they received after it had been inspected. Premade cards were given that said, "Thank you for the gift, and we are fine." Only a tiny bit of room was allowed to write something, but then it was read by the Nazis before being sent, so what could you write?

Seeing Terezin was a shock. There were wash sinks standing in a row, but there was no plumbing connected to these sinks. Had the Red Cross workers turned on a faucet during their inspections, they would have experienced no running water from these sinks.

Visiting Terezin is quite easy from Prague. Numerous tours include hotel pickup and drop-off. The museums and artwork are a must-see. During the time my mom was in Terezin, they presented the play *Carmen* to the Red Cross. Also her cousin, Dita Pfefer, was a performer in the children's opera called *Brundibar*. My mother enjoyed watching this very delightful play. It was a performance filled with hope. There were numerous understudies in this children's opera as the performers were shipped off to other camps. The costumes were made from the clothing of those who had passed. Nothing was wasted. It was the ultimate Potemkin village. The tour includes the costumes and detailed explanations of what the camp was like, but do bring Kleenex.

One of the most emotional things to see was the shower facility. Although they claim that these were not gas chambers, I wonder about the ability to substitute gas for water. The toilet consisted of a cut-out box that sat over a hole. It was a private toilet, unlike the facilities at Auschwitz which consisted of toilets in a row.

I remember how my mom explained that burning Jewish people in the crematory was very emotional because there would be sounds and then everything went quiet, followed by a horrific smell. Even when we went on the tour, a faint smell lingered in the air. Numerous Germans in the camp said there was never a crematory, but even on the tour you can sense that there was.

After the departure of the last transport from Terezin to the East (October 28, 1944), the SS staff began covering up the traces of their crimes in the ghetto. That same year, the SS ordered the ashes of the deceased prisoners to be liquidated. Approximately twenty-two thousand urns were emptied into the Ohře river, and another three thousand were buried near Litoměřice concentration camp.

Crematory. Yes, it really happened

The gentleman to the right is wearing a star designating him as an appointed supervisor by the Nazis.

There was no photography of any kind by the prisoners, but artists detailed their experiences with any marker, broken pencil, or coal they could find. To impress the Red Cross, the Nazis allowed art classes, but everything was taken away. My mom's art teacher in her hometown in Brno, Otto Unger, painted his experiences. The Germans found his work in the studio and moved him to be killed, but instead they decided to cut his fingers off. He survived the camps but died from typhus and exhaustion in Buchenwald only one month after being liberated.

This is one of Otto Unger's drawings.

There are not enough words to explain.

I was having dinner one night with my mom, and we were eating a lovely meal. Suddenly my mom froze, and I asked her what was going on.

She said, "Now I get it."

I said, "Get what?"

She explained that the carts that were used at night to take the burned bodies away were the same carts that carried the bread to concentration camp prisoners.

CHAPTER 5

Auschwitz

October 23, 1944. Musicians greet the transport to Auschwitz.

Upon entering Auschwitz, you were greeted by a beautiful orchestra playing music. These were very talented Jewish musicians—the best in their field. Once settled, Ruthie didn't hear much music anymore.

This was the worst camp ever, Ruthie explained. In the morning, you got up, went to a field, and stood silently to get counted. After a few hours, you went back the barracks and rested, only to get up and be counted again. Whatever items my mom had brought into Terezin were now long gone, and she wore striped clothing.

As soon as her group got off the transport, Jewish prisoners started cleaning it immediately. My grandmother recognized a Jewish prisoner, and he warned her that this camp had showers that doubled as gas chambers. This was the first they'd heard about gas chambers. Each time my mother got shaved and was told to shower, she prayed, knowing these could be the last few moments of her life.

Many times Ruth heard people line up to "shower," but then it got silent. Within days, Auschwitz smelled of darkness.

Food consisted of a powder soup and a piece of bread, maybe, along with water. Accommodations were very limited. My mom was separated from her mother for the first time, and no one had any idea where Oskar was. As my mom explained, as long as you were working or keeping busy, the days went by. But if you just had to stand there, not saying anything and being pushed around, this was the worst—just standing there and getting counted.

Barracks in Auschwitz

Six times my mother faced Dr. Mengele, the research doctor known for experimenting on twins and such. If he pointed to the left, you were safe, but if he pointed to the right, you were never seen again. Dr. Mengele saw you naked, and as I mentioned, my mom went through this process numerous times. As I have read about Dr. Mengele, it sickens me to know what he was capable of doing. The power this man had was unreal, and the decisions he made for those who survived were felt throughout their lives.

Richard Baer, Dr. Josef Mengele and Rudolf Hoess

My grandmother's sister, Elfie, did not feel well. My grandmother was most concerned about her dear sister, so she started to hit her cheeks a bit, trying to get her some color. Inside the barracks that winter, my mom and grandmother stood. This standing was called an "appeal." Everyone was nude during these appeals.

A surprise visit from Dr. Mengele came, and my grandmother was very nervous because the last thing she wanted to see was her sister facing Dr. Mengele and then being taken away. Erna looked all around and found a red wrapper from an imitation coffee product. My grandmother put this red on her sister's cheeks and kept hitting her face and rubbing it in until there was color and she did not look sick.

They got closer to Dr. Mengele. Aunt Elfie's daughter Dita survived by getting pushed between my grandmother's legs. The doctor kept on walking but never saw little Dita. That was a good day. All four ladies survived. As Dr. Mengele finished his search for victims, the fine ladies finished walking around in a circle, and then they got dressed and went to their bunks.

As my mom stood once again in the nude before Dr. Mengele, a miracle occurred, and she got transferred to Oederan, a camp that needed workers.

Toilets

My grandfather was completely humiliated in Auschwitz. He was given a tattoo number. As a child, I remember looking at this number, but he would change subjects when I asked him about it. I found it odd that he had a tattoo, but then again, I didn't know any better.

Before you read the next part, please take a deep breath and one minute of silence, not just for my grandfather but for those who suffered in Auschwitz and all other camps.

My grandfather had a dear friend, and somehow this man ended up with diarrhea. One thing about the camps—if you were not in perfect shape you would be killed, no questions asked. Even a bruise could get you shot because you were injured. A scar, missing teeth, or simply looking older was reason enough to put an end to life. So the Nazis threw this man onto a toilet and started to beat the crap out of him. As he lay on the floor in his own defecation, my grandfather saw what was happening and tried to save this man. It was too late for his friend, but now the Nazis started in on Oskar something fierce.

As he lay almost dead, a miracle of a Jewish supervisor walked in, cleaned him up, and covered his bloody cuts. This man found a way to get my grandfather transferred to a new working camp called Blechhammer. After Blechhammer, he went to Gleiwitz.

Looking at it now, my grandfather survived an extermination camp, not just a concentration camp. When Blechhammer was established in April 1942, it was known as a labor camp for Jews. When 120 prisoners contracted typhus, they were transferred back to Auschwitz, where they were killed. Some 200 female Jewish prisoners were put into a separate section of the camp. Hunger and disease were rife, especially diarrhea and tuberculosis. A crematorium was built in which were cremated the bodies of 1,500 prisoners who had died from "natural" causes or had been killed. Jews do not believe in being cremated, so this was a double insult.

Blechhammer in English means "sheet metal hammer." I asked my mom what my grandfather did in this camp, but she did not know. In my research, this camp was a gasoline plant that had numerous accidents and deaths. The first 3,056 male prisoners at Blechhammer had tattoos from Auschwitz—numbers 176,512–179,567. There were also 132 female prisoners—numbers 76,330–76,461. Prisoners declared unable to work were sent by the camp administration to Auschwitz II (Birkenau) to be murdered. Other "healthy" workers were then sent from Auschwitz to Blechhammer to take their place.

On September 9, 1944, American bombers destroyed large parts of the plants of the "Oberschlesische Hydrierwerke AG" in Blechhammer and of the oil refinery in nearby Trzebinia. On January 21, 1945, 4,000 prisoners—including 150 women—were taken out of the camp and put on a death march lasting thirteen days. Several dozen prisoners who tried to hide in Blechhammer during the evacuation were discovered and killed on the spot.

The prisoners each got eight hundred grams of bread, a small portion of margarine, and artificial honey for their march. Some eight hundred prisoners were killed en route. On February 2, 1945, the survivors reached the Gross-Rosen camp, where they remained for five days before being put on a train to Buchenwald on February 6 or 7. On the way, the train was attacked several times by allied planes, which caused many deaths.

The total number of forced laborers working in all camps at Blechhammer (not only the subcamp of Auschwitz III) and surroundings reached about forty-eight thousand people. This included two thousand British prisoners of war.

Oskar did not talk much about his experiences, although there were times you could see in his face how he suffered. Oskar was a true jewel and everyone loved him. I never saw my grandfather without his mustache, and there was never a spot of dirt on his car.

CHAPTER 6
The Artist

Kitty Brunnerová

Kitty and Eva Brunnerová were distant cousins to Ruthie. Their mother, Hilda, was second cousin to Oskar. As the story goes, little Kitty was an artist and loved to draw. Germans made silhouettes, and Jewish children painted them. Little Kitty took some items to draw with and stuck them under her pillow. No one knew about her drawings. She was put onto a transport to Auschwitz with her sister Eva. As her bed was being cleaned, Jewish people found her drawings.

One hundred children were put on a transport thinking that they would be exchanged for German prisoners who were in England. That was the rumor. My mother's dear friend Fredy Hirsch volunteered to go with the children to Israel. Instead, they all ended up in a family lager in Auschwitz. Fredy had a good rapport with the German overseers and believed the children would be saved. Instead, the Nazis killed the children. Fredy could not believe it. He himself committed suicide. When my mom returned to Terezin for the fiftieth anniversary of the liberation, they dedicated a memorial to Fredy Hirsch.

Years had gone by, and my mother went to Israel for the fiftieth anniversary of the Holocaust survivors. She was greeted by Shoshanna Newman, the aunt of these children. For many years, the father had pictures of his children in his coat pocket. He went to Israel (Palestine) illegally though Cyprus. Rumor has it that he swam there. At the time, this was part of England.

Kitty is on the right.

In Israel, Shoshanna handed my mother some photos and a letter. Because my mother was the last known relative, she wanted these photos to be safe and keep the memory of these children alive. My mother was not able to meet the father because he had died, but she met the mother.

As you can see, one of Kitty's drawings was made into a postage stamp in Czechoslovakia. Kitty's original drawings can be seen in Holocaust museums in Israel and in Washington, DC. The picture is of a cat jumping over a fence, trying to be free.

Try To Remember-Never Forget

My mother asked that I keep the memory of these children alive. I replied, "With pleasure."

CHAPTER 7

Oskar's Tattoo

M y grandfather had a favorite joke he liked to tell: An old Jewish guy in the United States won the Lotto jackpot of $120 million. While being interviewed by the local news, he was asked what he was going to do with the money.

"First thing I'm going to do is give half the money to the Nazi Party in Germany."

Somewhat surprised by this response, the news guy asked, "Why the hell would you do that after all the things they put you and your family through during the Holocaust?"

"Well, come on, fair's fair," he says as he rolls up his sleeve. "They did give me the winning numbers."

Rest in peace, Oskar.

I can't begin to tell you how many letters I have written to find documentation of things that have happened to my family. I was on a quest to find my grandfather's tattoo number and confirm it from a photograph, and I received this response:

26th August 2015
Dear Ms. Scheller,

Thank you very much for your message of today. However, I am very sorry to have to tell you that in our archival collection there are no documents informing about prisoner number of Mr. Oskar Goldschmied.

I would like to explain that in our archival collection contains only a very small part of whole documentation created in the camp offices during activity of KL Auschwitz (from spring 1940 till January 1945). The Nazis had destroyed the larger part of those camp files just before the final evacuation and liquidation of KL Auschwitz to efface the traces of their war crimes committed there. One part of those documents was also transferred to Germany. In addition, many of those files that had not been destroyed by the Nazis were taken over by the Red Army after the liberation of KL Auschwitz and transferred to the then Soviet Union. Therefore, at present we have the very serious problems with establishing the fate of many of the deportees because of the lack of any documentation. I am sorry to say that this is the case of your request.

I would like to suggest you contacting with your request The International Tracing Service in Bad Arolsen, Germany. Here is its address:

INTERNATIONAL TRACING SERVICE
Grosse Allee 5-9
D-34454 Bad Arolsen
Germany
Phone: 0049/5691 629 0
Fax: 0049/5691 629 501
e-mail: email@its-arolsen.org

I am very sorry that I am unable to help you with your request.

In our archival collection there are documents mentioning to two persons whose name was Oskar GOLDSCHMIED.

Oskar Goldschmied, born on 23rd October 1887, was deported to KL Auschwitz from the ghetto-town Theresienstadt or Terezin from the Czech Republic in the transport that arrived to Auschwitz on 16th December 1943. His further fates are unknown.

Oskar Goldschmied or Goldschmidt, born on 7th November 1913 in Mnischek, was deported to KL Auschwitz from the ghetto-town Theresienstadt or Terezin from the Czech Republic in the transport that arrived to Auschwitz on 29th September 1944.

On 10th October 1944 he was transferred from Auschwitz to KL Dachau. His further fates are unknown.

Yours faithfully

Wojciech Płosa, Ph.D.
Head of Archive
The State Museum Auschwitz-Birkenau in Oświęcim

CHAPTER 8

Gleiwitz

My grandfather was now in a working camp after being beat up for helping his friend as described in Chapter 5. He was able to consume more calories, meet new friends, and continue living one day at a time hoping that tomorrow would be a new day with a different way of living. As sirens blared, news got out that they needed to evacuate the camp. He and three friends went into a kitchen and hid in the kettles for twenty-four hours.

As the camp got silent, they slowly opened the lids of their temporary dwellings only to realize no one was there. They found clothes to change into, and now my grandfather, Oskar Goldschmied, was no longer a Jew in a camp. With his new clothes, he ran with his friends into the mountains, running at night and sleeping by day. It was an absolute miracle that Oskar was able to reunite with my grandmother's brother Manfred Konka. Manfred had avoided the camps by hiding and bribing. He was a Partisan and had received word from others as to what was going to happen to the Jews.

As my mom explained, she loved Manfred dearly; he was witty and an absolute genius. Most importantly, he saved my grandfather's life, giving him money, meals, and a place to stay. Manfred sold hunting coats, ties, and shirts, so he was able to trade for what he needed or wanted.

With the help of Manfred, Oskar was able to get sleep, food, comfort, and information about the future. He knew nothing about where Ruthie or his wife were, but his determination and his faith kept him. I can only imagine Oskar, with his full lips, singing under his breath every possible prayer, not having time to think about what had happened over the past few years.

Manfred got word that the Russians were invading and the Germans were running scared. Train tracks and bridges were now bombed out, so taking any form of transportation was not an option. It was, "Feet don't fail me now."

Here is Ruthie with Manfred and her cousin
just before the home invasion.

When I think of my grandfather walking from Gleiwitz to a noman's-land, I picture him with his hands behind his back or in his pockets, whistling a tune under his breath. This is what he did when I was young, and I can only imagine this is what he would have done then.

I was with my cousins Karel and Felix last year. These are the children of my grandfather's brother, Walter. We were walking on the pier in Imperial Beach, California, and the brothers were next to each other with their hands behind their back. I believe our group had to photograph this most wonderful moment because this was a Goldschmied trait.

My cousins, Dr. Felix Goldschmied and Karel Goldschmied

CHAPTER 9
Zamosc Ghetto

Vilem with his son, Gideon and wife, Kamila.
They dug their own graves.

As I mentioned in the beginning pages, my grandfather's brothers Vilem and Zigmund—and their wives and children—had to dig ditches and then were buried alive in April 1942. The Red Cross had lists of those who were killed.

Zamosc was once known for being a very religious Jewish community, but in the spring of 1942, the first mass executions of members of the Jewish intelligentsia accused of making contact with

Communists took place at the Rotunda in Zamosc. There were to be many further executions at the Rotunda. This was, by far, the bloodiest camp ever.

Ruthie told me that these two brothers were the most religious members of the family, and she had a hard time understanding how brothers who were so physically fit could end up getting killed.

To this day, Ruthie holds copies of the numerous German notation papers that explained each person's transport and camp destination. She obtained them when she went back to the camp and bribed a librarian to look the other way while she made copies.

CHAPTER 10

Oederan

(Flossenberg Jurisdiction)

October 27, 1944

After less than a week in Auschwitz, Ruthie was told to take a shower and was blessed to have water instead of the gas. She was given a used dress and a coat. At that point, she was placed into an open wagon and sent to another no-man's-land, but she got word that they were placing people to work in another camp. The first stop was Flossenberg, but it was overcrowded, so next was the working camp. Mom believes that had she stayed in Flossenberg, she would not be alive. The transport to Oederan took four more days.

My mom started out making bullets in the factory. She would walk and find sand and pick it up. When no one was looking, she would put the sand in the bullet machines and clog them up. She figured that this would make the bullets unusable and therefore would save a Jewish person from getting killed or wounded. Of course, no one saw her doing this.

My mom found different pieces of aluminum, and she made a Jewish piece of jewelry. Of course, no one ever found this star, and yes, we have it to this day. She also would take bread dough and make little tiny dolls and figures. We have these priceless treasures. At one time, some worms found their way into the dough, but for the most part, these items are recognizable. Ruthie made a cook and a Buddha. Yes, a Buddha! I need to build a Ruthie museum.

Here are some items that show what Ruthie made from bread dough and the aluminum that made the bullets.

There was not enough electricity in this camp, so my mom volunteered to lay electrical cable in the street in the winter. This was very hard work, plus it was cold.

Each week, the Nazis painted an X and a white stripe down the back of my grandmother's dress. Painting it was a form of identification, and I guess it was better than being tattooed. This was done because she didn't wear a uniform and could remain in her one single dress. If you look at the dress carefully, you can see openings in the hem of the dress where she had placed things that she found. I believe she even had gold teeth in it along with the wrappers she used to redden the face and cheeks of those who were pale and getting sick. Where is the dress? I have it, paint and all. It has been on display so many times, and now we are treating it like a child. My mom went to Washington, DC, thinking about donating it, but they have hundreds of such dresses in the basement.

One day my mom noticed a very quiet non-Jewish prisoner and wondered who this woman was and why she was in the camp. Again, everyone showered together, and my mom remembered this woman's body, so badly beaten on her back and her backside. As my mom explained, you could see hundreds of lashes on this woman.

She later learned that this woman's boyfriend was Jewish, and this was forbidden.

G-d rest your soul dear woman. You are not forgotten.

April 11, 1945

My mom remembers it well: As she was waking up, she was told to gather her belongings and go outside. There, Nazi youth with bayonets confronted her. She asked one of the youths how old he was because they all looked so young. Instead of working, she was now standing again, waiting to be counted. After the prisoners were counted, they were put onto trains and sent to Flossenberg (an extermination camp) but with the Russians liberating the area and the roads and bridges blown up, they were forced to walk. As they approached another train, they stood with their clothes on and were hosed down. This was their shower and clothes washing all in one.

The train stations had limited food, and there was a bucket on the train to eliminate body waste. This train held five hundred people— one hundred from Hungary, two hundred from Czechoslovakia, and two hundred from Poland. People lay on the floor at times because standing was difficult. "We made a deal that those standing would be laying and those laying would be standing every hour on the hour," she told me.

There was a Jewish supervisor who helped with this transport, which eventually ended up in Terezin. If anything went wrong, this supervisor, Edith, was to blame. My mom felt kindness from her, but she too was doing her job to make sure she was not hurt or killed. A German female guard got into a verbal match with my grandmother because she thought she overheard my grandmother saying something about where everyone was going. I believe that Edith was there to step in and make sure that my grandmother was not harmed.

My mom witnessed a Jewish prisoner seeing a Russian soldier and running toward this soldier. There was nothing the Germans could do. My mom explained that years later in America, she saw this woman and her sister. I believe that as my mom and grandmother walked and took trains, they may have believed there was an end to this concentration camp madness.

The roads were bombed out, and the bridges were broken. The Germans were running, and what Germans remained began to exchange their clothes with what was in their backpacks. Some even dressed as Jews in those beautiful striped outfits.

The Russian military fed people on the trains. Many people who were in the camps joined the military depending on who occupied them or freed them. The soldiers were nice to Ruthie, even giving her chocolate.

The Russians had invaded and were out for any Germans they could find. But there were those Russians who felt that since they had liberated the Jews, they were entitled to some of the women. Thank G-d my mom was not one of them. My grandmother took Ruthie and wrapped her in a blanket during this time, pretending she was a baby. Ruthie was a bit confused by this; she had no idea that freedom was just around the corner.

As they could no longer go by transport, they were forced to walk. The rails were bombed out, so they alternated between walking and riding in open wagons.

After two weeks of walking and riding broken trains, they ended up in Terezin on April 21, 1945. Imagine returning to Terezin! But this time things would be different. Mom was looking forward to getting back to Terezin so that they could eat and have a place to sleep. It was there that my mom saw her relatives, but because of the typhoid quarantine, they could not touch each other. No hugs, no kisses.

Oskar did not know that his wife and daughter had left Terezin in the first place. He looked through the Red Cross list and found their names. In the meantime, Mom and Erna registered to go to England as refugees working as housemaids.

A few days later, Oskar arrived at the gate. Mom was in the kitchen working and someone yelled, "Ruthie, there is someone at the gate who wants to talk to you."

She ran to the gate thinking it was a friend or an uncle because this man had no beard or mustache and was very skinny. But then he said, "Don't you know your own father?" There they stood, only able to see but could not touch because of the electricity running through the fence that separated them.

Ruthie ran to get Erna, screaming, "Papa is at the gate!" Once again, no hugs or kisses were allowed, but they were so happy to know he was alive.

CHAPTER 11

Reborn

Ruthie was in quarantine for about thirty days. On June 15, 1945, at six in the morning, someone came by and yelled that they were free to go and that they had to leave. All Ruthie could think about was going to Israel. The most important thing was to register with the Red Cross so they could be followed and family members could find one another.

So much hope was in the hearts of those who soon found out that someone had been killed or died. The Germans had everything so calculated and notated. They kept track of everyone they killed. With those lists to go by, the Red Cross was able to reunite families. All this was done without computers, just very neat note cards. My mom kept thinking that to get and give information as they did was a pure miracle.

Oskar came to pick them up on June 20, 1945. They drove home in military trains and traveled any way they could, depending on what was bombed. Normally it would take five hours by train, but this took three days.

Where does one get food or a place to sleep or money for anything? The only thing my mom had was a blanket. The lining of her coat had been used for sanitary napkins, but she had lost her period and the rest of the lining was made into a bra. As in a marathon race where stations are set up, the Red Cross greeted my mom and family, providing a meal here and a meal there, a bed here and a bed there. But with each day that passed, finding a place to eat and sleep became harder and harder.

When they found their way back to Brno, they went to their old home and saw that it had been made into offices by the Nazis. With his month's head start since he was not quarantined, Oskar had secured another apartment, although there was very little in it. A family with a daughter had formerly occupied the apartment, and this girl left behind many things. Ruthie was able to fit into this girl's clothes, and little by little, things started to come together.

Many items were given to them for free to make the transition easy. The first thing they were given was a pot, which was the only way to get soup. Ruthie remembers going into a hotel basement in Brno, across from the train station, where they were able to get soup for free. As weeks went by, she noticed that there were more things added to the pot, such as potatoes, leftovers, and canned foods, along with food from Russia and Poland. They had to go to the hospital to get vitamins, protein, calcium, pills to start menstrual cycles, and pills to remove water that had built up.

Oskar was unusually swollen, and this worried the family. He was hospitalized and given proper fluids and nutrition to return to normal. Although he got better physically, one questions the emotional ramifications of being a prisoner with hardly anything to eat, robbed of his wife and child, parents and brothers, love and support, passion for life, religion—all the things we take for granted. The sooner he could return to his past before the camps, the sooner he would heal both physically and psychologically.

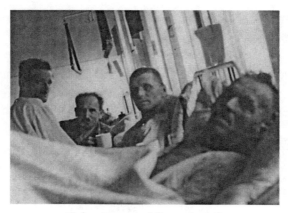

Oskar is second from the left

Upstairs in the hotel, they were given dry goods. The goal was to get as many towels as possible, although they only got one towel each. One thing I can say about my mom, she will starve herself to death if someone has not eaten before her. To this day she shares everything. I can't say that all survivors do this.

Before the camps, my mom went to a Jewish school. Upon returning, she was shocked to find out that this school had been turned into a dentist's office for the Nazis. After the war, my grandmother was able to go to this dentist's office, but she used her brother's identifying information which allowed her to get her teeth fixed for free.

Now, Ruthie went to a school for girls that taught ballroom dancing. The boys' school across the way also had a class in ballroom dancing. My mom went to the joint school dance only to see a sign that had not been removed—*Jews Forbidden*. She was furious and demanded to have these signs removed. No one did anything except promise. She stormed out of the school and demanded her money back. She told me her stomach burned with anger because of this.

Ruthie had missed so much school that she could not get into college to pursue her dream of being a clothing designer in Paris. She wanted to continue her studies in tailoring. She wanted to follow in her father's footsteps by working with clothing and fabric. She had a very artistic hand, and her sewing skills were impeccable. She has the patience of a saint and will stop at nothing when it comes to learning and bettering herself. I personally have witnessed techniques and ways of doing things that have not been seen by anyone else.

She went to a local designing school and studied the history and present design of clothing, along with immaculate hand-detailing. She graduated after three years with a diploma. I can only imagine her delight as she stayed focused on her studies and could forget her past for just a few moments. But the past never goes away; you just learn to live with it.

Had she continued her stay in Europe, I'm sure my mom would have worked in a fashion house, but after coming to the United States and sewing, she was a factory worker. She made our children's costumes and even my professional mime outfits, as well as most of our clothing. On the next few pages are clothes and designs by her.

Try To Remember-Never Forget

This is her personal monogram.

Ruth Sax was the second-place winner in the Singer sewing machine contest in beautiful downtown Chula Vista, California.

Sandra Scheller

Wearing the "pants" in the family

If my mom didn't sew and design her clothes, she had them made by famous Femina from Brno. Frances Grubner took her photographs.

As a child, I remember learning to knit and crochet, but when it came to sewing, my mom was too afraid of my breaking her machine. I'll never forget the day she got a new sewing machine. Here we are fifty years later, and she insists on keeping that machine alive. Now I sew for her. I'm sure that if she had the opportunity, she would, but her back is so frail. Honestly though, it is fun dressing my mom as she dressed us as children."

The wife of my grandfather's boss was an incredible seamstress and made nightwear and lingerie. I will say that to this date, I have never seen anything so beautiful as the hand-detailed nighties that my mom has saved.

CHAPTER 12

Tribute to Walter Goldschmied

Dear Walter,
Although I do not know you, I truly love my cousins Karel and Felix Goldschmied. We joke about being Schmiedsters. My mom told me so much about you and Auntie Gardie. I was shocked from all the stories to learn that you broke your back while a

chauffeur was driving a car and ran off the road. I learned you were in the backseat and while the others lived, you were in the hospital. My mom explained that your beautiful wife fed you home-cooked meals during your hospital stay. It had been about a month, and on one particular day, she had just fed you soup. By the time she came home, she had gotten word that you passed on.

Your picture was displayed in my grandfather's room as long as I can remember and until the day he died.

You created two beautiful children along with nine fantastic grandchildren and ten great-grandchildren. The Goldschmied name continues in Australia but remains in our hearts forever.

I visit your brother at his grave all the time in beautiful San Diego, California. I believe there is quite a Goldschmied party happening. Although I am a Scheller, please save a space for me, and we can all walk heaven with our hands behind our backs whistling.

CHAPTER 13

Skeletons in the Closet

*Suicide doesn't take away the pain;
it gives it to someone else.*

There are some things that are painful to talk about. One of my relatives committed suicide after the war. Rumor has it that my grandmother and my father found him on a door.

In Judaism, we do not believe in cremation or suicide.

This particular relative went through the camps. He was very successful before being put into the camps, and upon coming back he found everything a bit more difficult and very frustrating.

There is a saying that it is the first million that is hard to make; after that, it gets easier. In this case, it was the opposite. This cousin knew how to make money before, and getting established again was a lot harder.

His wife was very frustrated and hated being in Czechoslovakia. There was talk of them going to Israel, but the fear of failure was more than he could handle. I'm sure many things went through his mind—that maybe this could happen again, or that the memories would be just too much to bear.

To this day, I get sad knowing that he gave up way too soon.

*One wakes up every morning to face and fight the same
demons that left you so upset, frustrated and tired the
night before, and this, my friend is called, bravery.*
—*author unknown*

CHAPTER 14

Viktor Frankl

In the years after the war, Oskar and my grandmother's brother, Manfred, went into business together selling uniform shirts. These shirts were bought by the military. Without getting into too much detail, the country was divided up into many different sections. Unfortunately my grandfather's section was in the Russian sector, and his business was taken away."

After the communist system took over the private businesses, my grandfather was advised by a friend to get out and emigrate. The goal was to get into the American zone. This was accomplished with the help of Viktor Frankl whose brother Erna had once dated. He declared my grandmother mentally unstable and in need of hospitalization, which allowed my grandparents to get into the American zone and then emigrate. He saved their lives.

By that time, my mom was in the United States married to my dad. She was able to pay a farmer with numerous pairs of house shoes sent from the United States to let my grandparents stay in his one-bedroom rental. These house shoes were being sold to other people in the village.

Viktor wrote the book *Man's Search For Meaning*. I remember his coming to our house for Passover, and he took numerous napkins and drew on them. My grandmother and mother collected these napkins as though they were gold.

Sandra Scheller

Viktor Frankl's artwork at Seder time 1970

"If you can find meaning in your struggles—
No matter how bad—
You'll grow beyond measure."
"The meaning of life is to give life meaning."

CHAPTER 15

Kurt Sax

Kurt, age seventeen, playing the accordion as a teenager on the ship Conte Di Savona coming to America on September 15, 1939. He arrived in New York on September 23.

My mother was seven years old when she first laid eyes upon Kurt Sax. He was her second cousin through the Goldschmied side of the family. Her grandfather Josef Goldschmied taught and prepared Kurt for his Bar Mitzvah. As Ruthie explains, if Kurt wasn't boxing her, he was trying to kiss her.

Kurt's own father had died when he was fourteen months old. As a child, grandmother Sax told me that Kurt said "Papa" when his father, Siegfried Sax, was sick in bed and dying of pneumonia. He left behind another son, Hansel.

By the way, Kurt Sax is my father.

In 1949, Ruthie and Kurt got married and came to The United States of America. The newlyweds spent two weeks in New York and one week in South Carolina, stopped to meet relatives in Texas and ended up in San Diego, California. How did they do this? They took the bus.

Kurt and Ruthie remained a honeymooning husband and wife for sixty-three years. On May 11, 2012, he died in Ruthie's and my arms.

The Nazis threw my father out of Austria when he was seventeen. He ended up in Northern Italy. Every time someone had gone to visit America and returned, he would request phone books so he could look up people with his last name hoping that they were related.

He wrote numerous letters, and one fine day someone wrote him back saying that, although they were not related, she was so touched by this letter that they had turned it over to a temple. A gentleman named Mr. Isaac Potts and his wife Leah responded saying that they would sponsor my father to the United States. He went first to Baltimore, Maryland, and then Anderson, South Carolina. Another gentleman named Mr. Siegel even wrote a letter for my dad asking everyone to give him just one dollar so that he could start a business. In 1997, my father and Mr. Sam Siegel reunited. I grew up hearing this story about a stranger's giving my father a new chance at life.

Try To Remember-Never Forget

Here is my father's newsstand. We can call this his "humble beginnings" in Anderson, South Carolina.

Sandra Scheller

The following is from a newspaper article: "Max and Bess Siegel raised eight children in Anderson and, as each married, Max helped the newlyweds establish a business. His son Sam, in the years leading up to World War II, ran the Bern & Siegel Mule Company with his brother-in-law, Sam & Bern, and achieved some renown by offering a helping hand to immigrant Kurt Sax, who had fled German occupied-Austria in 1939 and landed in Anderson at age 19. Sam gave the needy and ambitious young man a dollar and a note to hand other local Jewish business-owners, urging them to do to the same. The assistance Kurt received enabled him to open a kiosk, where he sold a 'complete line of magazines, newspapers, soft drinks, cigarettes, cigars, tobaccos,' and gave him a kick-start toward a successful career as an executive in a large, well-respected company on the west coast."

Ruthie married Kurt on April 8, 1949.

If you look carefully, you can see that one of her feet is bigger than the other because she broke her ankle just before the wedding.

Although it is not talked about, my father was briefly married to someone else for a short time before he married my mother. I remember talking to him about the "other woman," and he was somewhat uncomfortable. Rumor has it that he was living with other relatives and they introduced him to this woman in the hope that he would move out and move on. After his divorce, he asked some relatives about that little girl he played with as a child. Ruthie had mailed a photo to a relative, and somehow he saw this photo.

From then on, they wrote letters. Soon he wrote her the immortal words, "Ruthie, would you marry me?"

My father returned to Czechoslovakia to marry the love of his life and came by ship on the Vulcania. Just as the ship was ready to sail, the crew went on strike. Instead of leaving immediately, it left a month later. The company paid for the passengers' meals, lodging, and clothes cleaning. Instead of leaving in three days, it took three weeks to settle the strike.

They remained in Czechoslovakia for four months so that Ruthie could get her passport. On the first night of their honeymoon, my parents saw a dog, and of course my mom was very scared, bringing up her childhood memories of a dog biting her. My father was trying to comfort her and went over to the dog only to get bit in the knee. One of two pair of pants that he owned had now been torn.

As they honeymooned, they were supposed to collect some money from a woman whose husband owed it to the family. As they got into a district that had numerous Russian soldiers, my mom told my father to start humming. My mom had permission to be there, but my father was an American, and he was not allowed. So he began humming and they looked into each other's eyes so that the Russians would leave them alone. As they got to their destination, the woman explained that her husband was not at the house, but she gave my mom the address to where he was. My parents walked to the address that this woman gave them, only to find themselves in front of a jail.

CHAPTER 16

Not So Nice

Told on August 30, 2015

My grandmother on my father's side of the family had five brothers and five sisters. One of the brothers was a very well-to-do doctor. On the one hand, he was kind enough to let my father stay with him for a short while, but on the other hand, he was very mean-spirited.

My mom explained that he was upset with my father because my dad sold insurance at night to people after work and would sleep in the morning. The doctor relative did not like this and called my father a loser. He had the audacity to write my mother in Europe and tell her not to marry my father because of this.

Later on, this relative divorced his wife of thirty-five years because she had cancer in the eye, and he was not about to take care of her or deal with her destiny. I remember this lovely woman but never knew what broke them up. I do remember she was very sad at times, and I saw her cry while talking to my grandmother.

Growing up, we did not see much of these relatives. In 1974, I went with my father to New York. We met this man and his new wife as they entertained us in their beautiful Manhattan apartment. They were very nice to us—maybe because my father had proved that he was successful both as a husband and a provider. Had I known this story, I believe I would have spit in his face.

Again, I am laughing inside because I am just amazed at the stories Ruthie tells.

CHAPTER 17
The American Dream

My grandmother on my father's side, Sophie Sax

Sophie Sax was unusually beautiful in her own way. Her nose was big, her ears were big, she had the hairiest legs and arms, but boy was she beautiful. Sophie was my father's mother. She lived in New York in a fur factory and slept with rats and mice. She had suffered without her son and now was coming to California.

Meanwhile, my mom and dad had saved everything they could to bring Ruthie's parents over to the United States. After surviving the concentration camps, I believe there was no way my mom would be without her parents. Oskar and Erna were unstoppable, and they knew they could provide an income and use the skills they had learned in Europe here in the States.

Now they were one big happy family. But the question arose: who was the better cook, Sophie or Erna? I do remember some competition, so I will choose the wisest way out and take the Fifth.

Ruthie, Sophie, Oskar, and Erna worked at the Ratner clothing factory in San Diego. They were part of a clothing assembly team. Later on, they made parts and pieces on commission. Ruthie did anything she could to get overtime, and she dedicated herself to saving money.

My dad worked at Davies Motors repossessing cars. Ruthie told me a story about when she and my dad were finally taking a vacation, but my dad had a habit of looking at every license plate. Sure enough, there was a car on the road that needed to get repossessed. My dad followed the car, and when the guy went into the house, my dad let the air out of the tires and made a quick phone call.

I was so blessed that because of Sophie, we spoke German in the house. Having the advantage of another language was quite unique. Sophie loved to play piano and was quite fantastic at it. She walked everywhere; Sophie could walk six miles in a day and think nothing of it.

My mom admitted to me that having Sophie in the house was a bit hard because she was so opinionated. Ruthie also would have liked more time alone with her husband. However, it was great having the extra pair of hands for cooking and playing with us. And Ruthie was quite kind about the fact that no matter what, Sophie was still Kurt's mom. Ruthie took care of Sophie unconditionally until she passed.

Ruth's parents, now in America

CHAPTER 18

Orange Belt Café and Oskar's Market

```
BETTER        NEW!         BETTER
       DELICIOUS  DIFFERENT
   GOOD FOOD SERVICE IS OUR BUSINESS
      American and Continental  —  Home Style
                    at the
      ORANGE BELT CAFE
   807 BROADWAY  —  Next to Broadway Theatre
      NOW UNDER NEW MANAGEMENT

   Merchants Luncheon . . . . 67¢ ) SERVED
                                   ) DAILY
   HUNGARIAN GOULASH OUR SPECIALTY
   including Soup, Vegetable and Coffee . . $1.00
         Your Patronage Greatly Appreciated!
```

My grandparents owned a cafe called the Orange Belt Café at 807 Broadway in San Diego. They were so impressed with a Hungarian restaurant in Los Angeles that they decided to do the same thing in San Diego. With the cafe's being so close to the Bank of America, the employees from this bank came to this cafe.

Sandra Scheller

New Café Offers Tempting Dishes
Southwestern Jewish Press, September 3, 1954, Page 8

Oskar Goldschmied and Kurt Adam have purchased the Orange Belt Café at 807 Broadway. Recent refugees from Czechoslovakia, they will serve Continental Food, specializing in Hungarian dishes such as Hungarian Goulash, Vienna Schnitzel, Gefilte Fish and other popular dishes.

The Orange Belt Café will open at 8:00 a.m. for breakfast, lunch and dinner. Special lunches are from 67 cents and dinners are a la carte.

As my grandmother was going through the "change of life," the demand for this restaurant became way too much for her. My mom told her parents that there was no way she would work in a restaurant. My dad helped out the best he could, but one thing about my father, he could not cook. I remember I was with my mom, and when we came home, the kitchen was full of smoke. He had tried to put matzo in the toaster. This is the same as putting saltine crackers in a toaster. They burn and smell the house up. I will say that my dad was a good provider but not a cook, no way.

Within months, the business was sold. San Diego lost one hell of a good Hungarian goulash.

Oskar's Market
(That's *Oskar's* with a *K*.)

Next, my grandparents opened a grocery store. The staff consisted of Oskar, Erna, my mom, and my dad. It was in uptown San Diego. Oskar had a friend, Lazar Barach, who lent him $2,500 to start this business. Lazar also had a grocery store and told Oskar he could do no wrong. Within a year, Oskar paid him back.

The store had fresh meat with a full-time butcher, and Oskar made deliveries. I believe they opened this market to make sure they would always have food and never starve again. His dear friend and customer was the famous boxer Archie Moore.

Happy times at Oskar's Market with Archie Moore

I only remember good times at the market until one day mom came home and was most upset. Someone had jumped the counter, pointed a gun, and robbed her.

Another traumatic incident from this time came on December 23, 1963. My mom and I had gone to pick up my dad at the grocery store. As we were driving on the freeway, I turned around to look through the back window, and I saw a car behind us speeding and weaving. I remember saying to Ruthie, "Watch out, Mom!" Sure enough, the car hit us from behind, and down the embankment we flew. We were struck by a driver who had polio and was driving with his polio hand so he could light a cigarette with his good hand.

I'm trying to remember the exact details of this crash. I know they took my mom away from me to the hospital. I remember sneaking in under Sophie's coat to see my mom since you had to be a certain age to visit patients. That was my mom. I needed to see my mom.

After that, Sophie was particularly important in our life, as now my mom needed help. I remember her cast that looked like a barrel from the top of her neck to her pelvis. That was her life for eighteen months.

Would things have been different if she'd had better nutrition in the camps? Maybe. What I do know is that my mom was never the same after that accident, although she tried not to show it. My dad thought she was a brave soldier, and he did anything and everything to relieve her pain. This driver was another form of Hitler, striking an innocent person for his own satisfaction of a cigarette.

If the driver in that accident is reading this today, here's a note: You will never know the pain and suffering my mom went through. I only hope you learned from your mistake. Currently Ruthie is in a wheelchair, and I blame you for this. She had a chance after the concentration camps, but you took this chance away. Ruthie is strong and can survive anything. You just made it that much more difficult.

Eventually, Oskar's Market was sold. My father wanted to get out of the grocery business. He was brilliant with figures and numbers. He proved to many that a career change was possible, even at forty. He became a very successful stockbroker. Some of the great benefits of his job were that he would reach company goals and be treated to a vacation with my mother paid for by the company. Ruthie could experience the joys of the world.

But there were things still unsettled in my mom's mind. She longed to return to her roots and see who she could connect with. I wondered many times what she was thinking of and if she remembered those horrific things that should never have happened to her or anyone, for that matter.

CHAPTER 19

Living

Ruth with a Baby Ruth

In 1952, Ruth Goldschmiedova Sax began her own family. She was a very enriched Jewish woman living seven miles north of the Mexican border in Chula Vista, California. She had found that in San Diego there were other Holocaust survivors, and so the New Life Club was formed in 1953. She was busy raising two daughters, taking care of a mother-in-law, and serving as president of the Sisterhood at Temple Beth Shalom and on the board for the Jewish Family Service.

Kurt worked as a stockbroker and continued to educate himself in Jewish songs, learning every Torah portion. They kept kosher. They still kissed and hugged and pretended that every day was their honeymoon. They traveled practically all over the world. One thing for certain, they were grateful for each day that passed.

My mom continued her incredible sewing and designing. I can say we had some pretty great costumes. When entering a contest, we pretty much always won a prize.

As my mom started to decline, everyone thought that my dad would outlive her. She became terribly ill, and we were told that she had two weeks to live. It was as if an hourglass with two weeks in it was staring us in the face. One doctor said that there was one ray of hope, but we had to get her to the hospital in La Jolla, California. There, Dr. Eric Adler saved her life. She was given a super-duper pacemaker with every bell and whistle imaginable.

Six months after this happened, my dad got sick and ended up in the same hospital that had told my mom she had two weeks to live. My mom and I went to the ICU and found the folks who had given her that news. They were in shock to see her up and about. She showed her gratitude and was hugged by the staff.

I believe that her best doctor is G-d. She has so many stories to share, and hopefully she will continue to be able to share and tell them.

CHAPTER 20

RIP Kurt

May 11, 2012

They had been married for sixty-three years when, in April 2012, my dad had a stroke. He forgot how to swallow, and each day that passed took him closer to his final resting place. I hated watching my father die. I knew that his death would change my mom forever. I remember being with her in her great big bed, watching her sleep without him, as he was in La Jolla Nursing. We joked that he always wanted to live in La Jolla, California, and once he was in hospice, he could say that he lived and died there.

It got to the point that I just could not let him be alone, so I slept on the floor under his bed for five days, watching his breaths get fewer and fewer. My mom would come at nine in the morning with clean underclothes for me, and she would stay with him until seven o'clock at night.

Putting someone in hospice is one of the hardest decisions anyone can make. Ruthie refused to believe that he was dying. I had never been this close to death. Watching every process that he went through made me stronger to help those who need some loving care and understanding. Michael Sternfield once told me that saying nothing at a time like this is always the best thing to do. Just be the best listener you can be.

The day my dad passed, a hospice worker asked if my dad wanted a massage. My mom and I just laughed. I know my mom wanted that massage; I doubt my dad cared, but we thought, *What the heck.* So the therapist took out some orange oil, and we watched her rub his hands and feet and body. We could see that he was getting more relaxed.

After that massage, we were told to open a window because she could tell his soul would soon leave him. Boy, was she right. From the time of the massage to the time my dad passed was two-and-a half hours.

It was the beginning of Shabbat on a Friday night. We said the Shabbat prayers. I rubbed wine on his lips and put a chocolate chip from a bagel on his lips. We watched him take fewer breaths, and then the breaths became shallow. He had three small breaths, and that was it.

I believe to this day that my mom still has not cried. I can say that the day my dad died was the day she stopped using the walker and started using the wheelchair full-time. Although this was the end of my dad's life, it was now the beginning of a new family without Kurt. My mom needed so much help but just didn't know where to begin.

Even with Alzheimer's and a stroke, my dad knew my mom until the very end. Thirty minutes before he passed, he said "Amen." He got his wish, to pass on Shabbat. He felt that this was the holiest of holy days in Judaism. His passing was very gentle, and he died holding my mom's hand and mine.

At the time, we were Skyping with my cousins in Australia, Pam and Felix Goldschmied. He died as we Skyped. I was so lost as to whom to call and what to do. We made a call to Am Israel, the burial home, and they came to take my father on his new journey. I felt as thought I were in The Wizard of Oz, coming to the end of the yellow brick road as we said good-bye to my father.

As family members gathered at my parents' home, there was a feeling in the air that things just were not going to be the same. A part of me had passed, and I believe that my mom felt the same. To this day, I feel that he is just in the room next door.

Ruthie was hurting because she missed Kurt dearly. Many things happened the night he died, and Ruthie has said many times that I have become my father in many ways, taking on responsibilities that were never supposed to be mine.

My life was being a wife, a mother, a performer, a seamstress, a manager of a flying trapeze company, a dancer, and a musician. Now I was about to embark on the hardest job in my life, being a true daughter who would guarantee to the whole family that Ruthie would have the best life ever and that everything would be completely understood by her. I would only do what was best for Ruthie. Our life became filled with insurance companies, financial advisors, attorneys, and real estate agents.

More things got buried besides Kurt. We buried the things that emotionally crippled us so that we could enjoy life to its fullest. Instead of cleaning the yard, we go to the beach; instead of cooking and cleaning, we go out. Every day is a holiday. After his passing, when we went out, we would pretend that my father was still with us. For a while we took along a necktie and placed it on an empty chair. We visit his grave all the time.

CHAPTER 21

Ruthie's New Life Without Kurt

One thing about my father, he was an impeccable dresser. When it came time for his passing, he was ready with his prayer shawl and head covering.

Leaving my mother's side was not an option for me. I stayed with her to go through the mail, pay bills, and get a clue as to what was going on. My mom needed to see different doctors, and she was in such back pain. She was on prescription painkillers, and trying to communicate with her about them was next to impossible. To this day, I can't believe I threw all of her pain pills in the toilet and flushed. I thought she would kill me, but she remained silent. I took my mom back to the different doctors as she explained where her pain was coming from.

My mom still was living at home, but one of the caregivers got a little sassy. It wasn't until a dear friend called me on the phone saying that my mom looked "terrible" that I noticed. I guess I had spent so much time with her that I just didn't stand back and notice that she had bruises that were covered up and that she had lost so much weight. I thought that the weight loss was because of my mother's not enjoying meals without my father, but in reality, the caregiver took the money I gave her for shopping and spent it on herself.

Later on, we found out that the food she cooked for my mom was food she was preparing for her dogs in Tijuana. I had cornered her, asking why my mom had bruises and what was the story with the drastic weight loss. She didn't like my confrontation, and I fired her. It was brought up that my mom had lent her money, and she was kind enough to return the money. I guess having her driver's license and information helped in making a report if I had to.

We located a lovely home that boarded elderly folks, but this house became a dog- and -pony show as well. Their solution to having a house full of people with dementia was to give them wine all the time. My mom was and is not a drinker, so she found herself all alone as others were talking to the walls. The facility had a policy that you had to be in bed by seven o'clock at night, and this just was not Ruthie. Also, the dementia patients would wake and walk the halls during the night, banging on the doors and waking my mom. It took my mom three months to tell me how bad this home was, comparing it to a concentration camp.

We went to visit my mom's neighbor of forty-plus years who was in an assisted living facility. Within thirty minutes of leaving the facility, we had my mom signed up. As I rolled my mom to the different places in the facility, numerous people commented on my mom's Jewish star. Little by little, people were coming out of the woodwork and telling my mom that they were also Jewish. Now the facility has Friday night services and makes it a point to make foods for the different holidays, such as latkes for Chanukah or matzo during Passover.

Ruthie loves this place, and I know they love her. She used to swim in the Olympic-size saltwater pool and take a Jacuzzi, and each meal is great.

In March 2014, we accepted an offer we could not refuse and sold my mother's home. She donated the furniture and old clothes to the needy in Tijuana. The person who bought her home fell in love with my mom and even called her mama. We left the piano, and I believe that the new owner's children are taking lessons. We are hoping they are enjoying the orange and lemon trees Ruthie took such pride in growing. She asked the new owners if she could stop over and pick an orange every now and then.

As selfish as this sounds, it was relief to have the house sold. I had started to hate that house. It was empty, and the only reason for going there was to do stuff. Now I can spend more time with Ruthie. She can go everywhere except in sand and doesn't like rolling on a pier, although she loves sitting at the beach. Ruthie's time is spent with fellow residents and friends from the community and her past. She write letters, watches the market, plays bingo, takes an exercise class, and makes jewelry. She loves getting her nails and hair done.

Doing this book has been quite emotional for her. After telling me the things that happened in her life, she wakes up at night thinking about the wonderful relatives, aunts, and uncles who loved her so much.

Sometimes when I go to see her, she is in her room looking at the photos of Kurt and her parents on the wall. We have a thing that we do- we have a drive-by visit to the cemetery. We take my dad's favorite soda or chocolate, and we throw this on his grave. We kiss rocks and place them on the gravestone. We visit her parents, who are next to Kurt. We do this at least every two weeks.

Ruthie enjoys exploring different restaurants. She has experienced new foods such as sushi, Vietnamese, etc. I have noticed that she is not eating as much, but then again, she says that she wants to get in shape.

With David Reicks and my husband

CHAPTER 22

Reincarnation

The greatest gift I got from Ruthie was learning when to walk away from situations that are uncomfortable or when enough is enough. I faced one of these situations with my former boss who, I believe, was Adolf Hitler in a past life. I also believe that Hitler was so evil he formed himself into another life here on earth, becoming the boss in our department. Each and every day was a challenge, although I would never let on the problems and frustrations because it was a job that many wanted. I question what lessons we learned from the past, and was it possible to really have a Holocaust all over again?

Without going into much detail, I found that the worst characteristic of my ex-boss was his lying. He would say and promise one thing but do another. Also, he gossiped to me about other employees, and I would think to myself, I can only imagine what he is saying behind my back to others. Ruthie taught me a valuable lesson, it is none of my business what others say about me.

I was very afraid of this man because I saw what he did to some of my coworkers, and although my heart broke for one of them, I could do nothing. I could not get involved. I had to learn to play stupid and fast. The boss was very smart and had years of experience degrading employees. The best thing to do was to stay clear.

My coworker had to dodge verbal bullets from the supervisor.

The situation got so out of hand that she complained to human resources. Instead of getting to the heart of the matter, our boss poured salt into her emotional wounds by telling her she was not up to speed in her sewing skills and that everything was her fault. That is how the meeting began. Naturally, she was so belittled that she broke down and cried, unable to verbalize her feelings. If he didn't like her sewing skills, why didn't he mention it sooner instead of waiting until a meeting that was supposed to get the devil to stop throwing things and verbally bullying employees?

I remember coming to work, and the devil was on employee leave because of some photos that were not suited for coworkers. Needless to say, the coworker who complained had to live in fear as well. The boss did everything to defend the devil, but little did he realize his coworkers had so little respect for him. I made it a point to call him by his last name because he did not deserve my friendship after what he did. If the supervisor was spoken to, the boss considered it a learning experience for him, and he was not written up nearly as often as he should have been.

Each week it got worse and worse to the point that we no longer felt we owned our own souls as they had been sold to the devil. But, I can say that I did meet some great people there. But if I had to do it again, I would have quit sooner.

One day I went to work only to find a dancing rabbi and a Star of David on my sewing machine. My friend and coworker at the time thought these were cute, and personally, so did I. The boss grabbed his little black Hitler book to write me up. I explained that I did not put this star or the dancing rabbi on the machine. I was asked to remove them because they were religious items and we could not have these in the workplace—although taking two weeks to decorate our department in Christmas lights was completely acceptable.

A dancing rabbi, of course, is no more a religious item than the mechanical Santa in the shopping mall. Don't get me wrong, I like Santa Claus. He reminds children to behave. The Star of

David—that is a shield, a sign of protection in the biblical days, and it was a very sweet gesture that my coworker wanted me protected from the forces of evil. It means that in my heart I am connected to the Torah and I understand, to the best of my ability each day, that I have one G-d and one G-d only.

I think about my mom and my grandparents wearing their star that the Nazis forced them to wear, and I can't imagine a day going by that I don't think about what my family has been through. A Star of David keeps me very humble. It gives me hope.

As Christmas came, the boss cornered me in the parking lot, letting me know that I had Christmas presents waiting for me. I told him that I did not want them and that he could donate them to a worthy organization that would appreciate them. He then proceeded comment, "Is this your way of saying f—k you to me?"

My answer was no, I just didn't celebrate Christmas. My employee friend called me two hours later as the boss had explained to her what he had said. Of course I could have gone to human resources, but what good would that have done? Not a damn thing.

The following year, the boss announced that he was not giving Christmas presents but would make a donation to the animal society. Gee, I wonder if there were any Jewish dogs?

The worst thing was the stench. Just under my sewing machine was a sewer trap. Gas fumes would come through, and it smelled like rotten eggs. I remember all of us getting sick one day, and I grabbed bleach to get rid of this smell because we knew the smell was not right. My husband told me that bleach would kill the bacteria, and it did.

I still have the e-mail from the operations management telling me the smell was nothing to worry about and not to throw bleach. So I guess feeling dizzy, being sick to my stomach, and having a headache was nothing, right? No one wanted to go above anyone's head for fear of getting it chopped off. Hmm, reminds me of the gas chamber in Auschwitz, except Auschwitz didn't have a smell that made you sick.

I told my mom about this problem, and she said to be thankful that I had a job. Yes, I was dying to have this job. One evening, the smell got so bad that performers threw up all over the bathroom. I'm not sure what was worse, them or the drain.

I remember having long talks with my mother about the anti-Semitism and the working conditions. Together we agreed that this little Jew was not sticking around for the sewer gas chambers any longer.

Just before I quit my job, I threw up for two days and then had the strength to say I quit. As I exited the basement doors in my place of employment, I vowed to myself that my life would be dedicated to my mom and her needs along with continuing as an artist for people to enjoy. As the boss escorted me to the final door that I would never have to walk through again, he began to tell me that he, too, was not far from leaving and would retire. I believe he will have a hard time living with himself when he thinks about what he did to so many. After all, Hitler committed suicide when he knew he was failing.

Two weeks after I quit, the boss texted me with a friendly message. I did not reply. One week after that, I got the same message wanting to know if I got the message. Once again, there was no reply from this Jew. Silence is golden.

Do I miss the backstabbers, the bullies, and the coworkers who think they know it all? Do I miss the fact that I'm not with people who work all day, go home, sleep, and then do it all over again with a vacation now and then? Not really.

I am busier now than I have ever been, and I'm breathing air that actually is pleasant, surrounding myself with wonderful friends and family who know the meaning of life. My favorite saying is, "I can only please one person at a time, and today is not your day, maybe tomorrow." Thank G-d for tomorrow. Actually, thank G-d for today.

As I look for gratitude in all that I have, my husband reminds me "to want what I have and not have what I want."

I know in my heart I have an amazing family and am blessed with a miracle Mom. But I also know that one day, she will say her last words, give her last hugs and kisses, and even hear for the last time, "I love you."

I had to learn this somehow, and I'll give credit where credit is due. I guess you can say I went to UCDS (University Cirque Du Soleil) and know that things can only get better, not worse.

The following e-mail is proof that there really was a nasty smell coming from the drain. At the time this e-mail was written, the boss was sitting over the drain. Within that year, he and his assistant moved to another location, and yours truly sat over this drain. I guess maybe I should not be upset with him because the fumes had polluted his brain.

I believe fumes and chemicals got to Hitler, although rumor has it that Hitler had syphilis as well.

So many employees complained, but not one came forward except me. This is as far as it got, but had I gone to human resources, I know that would have been the end of my career. No matter how talented you are, complaining will be your enemy forever. As my mom reminded me, there were many people in her life who probably are reincarnated. Then again, Jewish people do not believe in reincarnation. So the best idea is to let it go.

As for the technical director, bleach does kill sewer-gas smells. I know I'm not supposed to know this, but being married to a physician verified this for me. As far as the boss, he always said that I should write a book. Maybe one day I will. Wait, I did.

Try To Remember-Never Forget

Message   Page 1 of 2

From:
Sent: Monday, March 17, 2008 5:17 PM
To:
Cc:
Subject: RE: smells in wardrobe

Yes, I can follow up. It would be helpful if I knew WHO in Prop Ops you've dealt with so far. The M-F, daytime supervisor that gives us the most attention is ▮▮▮▮▮. Has it been him? Also, I'll come down tomorrow and see exactly which drain you're talking about.

FYI, I wouldn't waste the clorox. If the liquid is seeping out of the trap, it's just, well, leaking out and not doing any good. The key to keeping (sewer) smells from coming up through the drains is to keep the p-trap full of water. When drains are not used (or plugged), that water in the p-trap evaporates and the seal is lost and the smells start seeping in. If there's a leak in the p-trap and it can't hold water anymore, no amount of liquid you dump into the drain is going to help it. Water is fine for dumping in the drain. Clorox doesn't really add any value.

Technical Director

From:
Sent: Mon 3/17/2008 1:09 PM
To:
Cc:
Subject: smells in wardrobe

Hi ▮▮▮

We are getting that awful smell down here a lot lately. One of the issues is the floor drain (capped) that is right by my desk. ▮▮▮▮ has addressed this with Prop Ops and they looked into the problem. It seems that the drain leaks and it is dropping down into the ground so that it is no longer flush with the floor. They have said that they will come in to fix the problem but so far nothing has happened. Would you mind putting this on your follow-up list?

When the smells get bad during the day Sandy pours water/clorox onto the drain, it quickly seeps down into the floor, and the smell seems to decrease. It is very odd to me that you can put water onto a sealed floor and it drains away. There must be a larger problem going on here.

Head of Wardrobe

3/25/2008

CHAPTER 23

Being Honored by So Many

With Ringmaster Johnathan Lee Iverson

Documenting my mother's stories has been a challenge. Since she moved from her home to assisted living, we have been attempting to put everything in order so that future generations can benefit from the life experiences of the Goldschmied and Sax generations.

One person I reached out to was Mary Salas, an assemblywoman when my parents were honored and now the mayor of Chula Vista, California. She sent the following letter:

August 26, 2015

Dear Sandy,

I remember your mother and father so well! They came to the State Capitol to be honored as part of the Holocaust Remembrance in April or May of 2009. My staff took many beautiful photos of the both of them that day. I also gave them a framed proclamation. It's quite large if she still has it.

Though it's sad to hear of Kurt's passing I am happy you still have Ruth.

I was looking through some old files but could not find the pictures or the program when they came to visit in Sacramento. I will continue my search.

If your mother is up to it, I would like to stop by soon to pay her a visit. If not give her a big hug for me.

Mary Salas

Ruthie enjoys meeting young students and reminding them that this cannot be allowed to happen again. Along the way, she has received numerous awards, letters, cards, flowers, and tears from students who found her story incredible and moving.

In the past, Ruthie attended gatherings of victims in Terezin and Auschwitz, but now, with her inability to walk, it is nearly impossible to travel. Also, the last thing we need is for her to fall ill and pass in one of those places. I would never be able to forgive myself for letting her go. But if she really had the desire to do this again, I would make it happen.

My parents were honored by an organization in Israel. They were very involved in raising funds and bonds for Israel. Here they are with Jonas Salk and Françoise Gilot.

In the summer of 2014, I got into a conversation about Ruthie with my dear friend Johnathan Lee Iverson, ringmaster of the Ringling Brothers Circus. He was so taken by Ruthie's history that he insisted on meeting her immediately. We went to visit her that night; she was in her pajamas and wrapped in a blanket as she talked with him. The next day, she got a call from the Ringling school inviting her to give a lecture to the Ringling students about the Holocaust. The students had the opportunity to think about what they wanted to ask her. The lecture was followed by a special tour just for her.

During Chanukah, Johnathan sent the most beautiful bouquet of fruit and balloons. It was so big that it almost didn't fit through her doorway.

Ruthie can say she has worked in a circus. Students from Ringling Brothers signed a painting created by an elephant with a paintbrush in his trunk. This priceless treasure hangs in Ruthie's room.

Boxes are filled with hundreds of letters from children from all over. Numerous letters include artwork from children drawing her as a lecturer or of something that happened in the camp. I have tried to discard them, but each and every letter and drawing is treated with respect and love. I see to this day her love for educating, communicating, and reminding everyone that what happened to her could happen again.

Ruthie is holding a survivor's candle. It is held with pride, but she is holding it high as she remembers her loved ones who didn't make it.

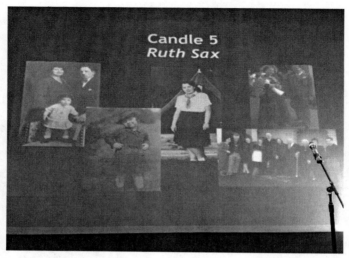

During the ceremony, you can see that there was a Ruthie moment for everyone to acknowledge her journey.

Max and Rose Schindler, with Ruthie, stay bonded as survivors. Rose and Max continue to educate the world about being a survivor. Ruthie is somewhat limited in her speaking engagements, although she has never said no to a group of young people wanting to know about the Holocaust.

Ruthie pictured with Rose Schindler and Roxanne Schindler Katz. We grew up together as children, and I cherish our friendship because of our bond as second-generation survivors.

Try To Remember-Never Forget

Then and Now

Here are images of before and after the camps. Can you find Ruthie?

Just after the camps. Ruthie and her childhood friend Frances Nassau are eating grapes. Seventy years later, they are in Sherman's Deli in Palm Springs.

Try To Remember-Never Forget

Before the camps, Oskar's clothing company.

Oskar's grocery store in San Diego, California.

CHAPTER 24

Hail to the Queen

Upon entering Paradise Village in National City, California, Ruth was greeted with such friendliness that it was hard to believe a facility could be this great. Paradise Village focuses on maintaining a community feeling, not a facility. She always repeated to herself that she wished Kurt could see this place and that this place is now her home. She was also near her neighbor of forty-plus years.

On Friday night, she was overwhelmed to see that Paradise Village offered Shabbat services. It was quality over quantity, and Mom began to meet some new folks who had something in common—Judaism. I remember going to the first service with her. Within minutes, the voices of seventy-five- to ninety-year-olds filled the room. Challah and wine followed. There was a group of women who lived in the independent part of Paradise, and they enjoyed baking for Shabbat. It was our first time trying chocolate chip cookies made with potato chips.

I've noticed that my mom openly wears her Jewish star on her neck along with my dad's wedding band. More and more people come out to meet, dine with, and eventually pray with her. Within six months of her arrival at Paradise Village, the director made an announcement that there was a new queen. My mom had no idea what the woman was talking about, but then her name was called, and shouts of joy filled the room. February 14, 2014, my mom was crowned the queen of Paradise Village. We just cannot say enough kind words about this incredible facility.

Mom was treated to roses, and she rolled in her wheelchair on a red carpet. There was a high tea and handmade desserts for this special event. I actually cried as everyone applauded for her because I doubt anyone knew what my mom has been through.

Although she thinks about her home of forty years, she knows that it was impossible to keep up. This way, we have more time to be with her instead of dealing with home duties and expenses.

CHAPTER 25

It's Not Your Time

I thought in April 2015 that I was going to lose Ruthie. She had a team of twenty-one doctors who said that they just didn't have a clue what her problem could be. She became very swollen in the face and throat and no longer had the strength to stand, talk, or even sit up. She could not remain at Paradise Village and now was in a rehab center with physical therapists working with her every day.

The daytime was great as different people worked on her strengths, but the nighttime was like a concentration camp as her fellow roommates with dementia crawled out of their beds and attempted to pull the covers off Ruthie. Of course, complaining did not help because there were no nurses around to complain to. They also thought she was having bad dreams and was making this up.

I remember staying with her one night, and the yelling of the people next to her and in the halls was horrible. It took a miracle to bring this horror to an end.

Try To Remember-Never Forget

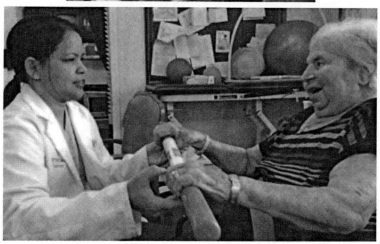

I called the Goldschmieds in Australia and my cousin Vera Hartford in Oakland, trying to figure out what to do. Vera wrote an e-mail to my cousin in Germany, and within hours, I got a message back from him that helped us put together a team of experts from UCSD. My mom has a special transport to and from the different doctors, and each and every transport was friendly and encouraging to her recovery.

I believe that the best medicine was a surprise visit from the Aussies. She had seen Felix and Pam about a year before, but she hadn't seen Karel and Frida in more than thirty years. As I watched her eyes and her expression, I believe the visit shocked the illness right out of her. Each day that the relatives visited her, she became stronger and stronger.

Each and every day, more and more people came to visit my mom. I believe that my mother was never alone in the daytime as more family, friends, and temple members came to see her. We even brought sitting chairs from home into her room.

She became friends with so many patients that when she was able to get back to Paradise Village, she felt sad to say good-bye. One thing I learned was that no matter where Ruthie goes, it is always home, and one needs to make the best of any situation.

CHAPTER 26

Ruthie's Temple

We grew up five miles from the Mexican border. Chula Vista's nickname was "ChulaJuana." Although English was the official language, life was much easier if you knew Spanish.

I was very surprised to learn that many concentration camp survivors lived in San Diego County. Many Jews who had tried settling in the United States ended up in Tijuana. Many smart immigrants started businesses that involved paying on credit, and slowly they enjoyed a nice life with beautiful weather among other Jewish people.

My parents had been members of their temple for more than fifty-eight years. My dad was the president at one time, and my mom was the president of the Sisterhood. Not only is this her temple; it is home. The building and her friends mean so much to her. I believe she is the only original member since the temple started back in the fifties. Many rabbis have come and gone, but one thing is certain- you can always find Ruthie seated next to her friend Shirley Garske in the front row.

I am so impressed by my mom's love for the temple. How difficult it must be to pray to G-d when G-d let her down so many times in the past. Maybe her past letdown is what gives her strength now.

CHAPTER 27

Who Is Ruthie?

Ruthie today is a truly fearless person. She is not afraid of anyone or anything and will voice an opinion without hesitation. She has so much love to give. I'm living with a new mama because this is not the mother I grew up with.

I am so fortunate to be able to talk to my mom two or three times a day. Instead of going through the normal, "Hello, how are you?" we cut right to the chase. Within one minute of our conversation, I know how she is feeling, what she is thinking about, and what her needs are.

As I look at boxes, folders, and documents, I can see my parents' lives unfolding right before my eyes. Now it will all get packed up for the next generation—or hopefully a Holocaust museum.

There are so many questions that will never be answered, but hearing my mom open up about the camps has been a true eye-opener. Lately I see more sadness as she talks, and it reminds me of someone digging a deep hole. Just when you think you have heard enough, there is more coming out.

Ruthie's mind is sharp as a tack, and you can't fool her about anything. I thought today that my mom looked spectacular, and I mentioned to my husband that I believe she is going to live forever. But the reality is that one day there will be a final sunset, a final curtain that closes on the grand finale of her life.

With my dad, I could see it coming. His last five days were hell on earth. But I believe that Ruthie will make her exit with style and grace. At the moment, she is not ready to even think about this ordeal.

I wondered how my mom felt about Germans now. I even asked her if she forgave Hitler. Her response blew me away. The people who hurt her are gone, and the children of the Germans have been so apologetic to her. If she were to hold a grudge now, she would create a concentration camp of hatred inside herself, and this is not how she wishes to live. She told me that there are German children who have hated their parents for what they did during this time. Ruth Goldschmiedova has the strength to forgive, and she hopes that those children can too.

My mom is pictured with Nicole Von Gaza Reavis from Butte, Montana. Nicole is the daughter of a Nazi who was captured in France. Nicole and I sewed together for a year. She is a daughter of a Nazi, and I am a Jew, and yet we are dear friends. Her moving away was so painful, but we make it a point to see each other and get acquainted with each other's friends and family. As they say in *Aladdin*, "It can be done." Nicole's father kept a detailed diary of his capture, which my mom was able to glance through.

EPILOGUE

And So It Is Written

As we continue the legacy of Ruth Goldschmiedova Sax, we must take a few moments to reflect within ourselves and embrace who we are and what we have.

It is my mission to continue helping not just my mother but other holocaust-survivor friends at the San Diego New Life Club sponsored by Jewish Family Service of San Diego. I have been to their celebrations of birthdays, anniversaries, memorials, and gatherings. David Reicks from Merill Lynch, San Diego, and his team of experts are advising me in helping to raise funds so that other survivors can enjoy life to their fullest.

Joining me in my mission is Etherial's creator and founder, Marcus Platrides from Cyprus. He is a renowned award-winning jewelry designer. Marcus has brought to life a pendant inspired by this book. This amazing piece represents the dress given to Ruth's mother in Auschwitz by the Nazis and marked on in Oederan. This custom piece is a reminder to spread the word to *never let this happen again*.

Proceeds will be donated to Jewish Family Service of San Diego. For more information, please visit www.etherial.eu.

Today marks the seventy-seventh anniversary of the invasion and my grandmother's birthday. As of this date, March 14, 2016, Ruth Goldschmiedova Sax is alive and well living at Paradise Village in National City, California. Although she thinks about her past, she still has a lot to look forward to.

If you wish to stay in touch with Ruthie, you can e-mail her at ruthgoldschmied@gmail.com. I can be reached at sscheller@cox.net.

Whatever Ruthie wants, Ruthie gets. Why not? She made me. Thanks for reading. And please—*never forget.*

ABOUT THE AUTHOR

Photo by Ed Foster

Sandra Scheller's artistic life includes creating and designing costumes and clothing for film, theater and runway. Her designing and sewing skills came from her mom and from her studies with flamenco costume designer Vera Ray in the United States. She assists Vilen Golovko of The Flying Cranes aerial ballet and trapeze for over seventeen years, with acts in Cirque Du Soleil and Ringling Brothers Circus, China, Germany and Russia. Numerous CD music covers—including Los Romeros and Ninel Novikova—feature Sandra's photography. She worked nine years at Cirque Du Soleil as a technician in wardrobe, and coached performers in and was head of wardrobe for Cirque Du Monde. In addition, she performed in a solo show at Marta Becket's Amargosa Opera House in Death Valley Junction, California. Sandra was nominated as the Artist of the Year in the state of Nevada 2010. She graduated from San Diego State University and received her teaching credentials from UCLA. She won the Top Female Mime Award at the National Mime Festival in 1975 and 1976, performed in numerous commercials as a mime, guest performed in Reading Rainbows and Sesame Street along with dancing with Rayna's Spanish Ballet. She is married, has raised two boys and now assists with the needs of her mom, a job and responsibility that takes priority over everything.

Sandra asked her mom if she was comfortable talking about her concentration camp experiences since it was not talked about when she was a child growing up in the Sax household. Her work in documenting her mother's life story is nothing short of miraculous because she was able to understand firsthand about Ruth's childhood while teaching us to NEVER FORGET.

CPSIA information can be obtained
at www.ICGtesting.com
Printed in the USA
FSOW01n0827240317
32211FS